DECADES OF HATS

1900S TO THE 1970S

Schiffer Publishing Ltd

4880 Lower Valley Road • Atglen, PA 19310

*To my late husband Jim
who was my greatest supporter
and the wind beneath my wings.*

Other Schiffer Books by the Author:

A Dandy Guide to Dating Vintage Menswear: WWI through the 1960s. Sue Nightingale. 978-0-7643-3890-8. $49.99

Other Schiffer Books on Related Subjects:

Women's Hats of the 20th Century: For Designers and Collectors. Maureen Reilly & Mary Beth Detrich. 978-0-7643-0204-6. $49.99

Baker's Encyclopedia of Hatpins and Hatpin Holders. Lillian Baker. 978-0-7643-0485-9. $39.95

High Fashion Hats, 1950–1980. Rose Jamieson and Joanne Deardorff. 978-0-7643-2450-5. $29.95

Type set in Anna BT/ Cambria

ISBN: 978-0-7643-4511-1
Printed in the United States of America

Published by Schiffer Publishing, Ltd.
4880 Lower Valley Road
Atglen, PA 19310
Phone: (610) 593-1777; Fax: (610) 593-2002
E-mail: Info@schifferbooks.com

For our complete selection of fine books on this and related subjects, please visit our website at www.schifferbooks.com. You may also write for a free catalog.

This book may be purchased from the publisher. Please try your bookstore first.

We are always looking for people to write books on new and related subjects. If you have an idea for a book, please contact us at proposals@schifferbooks.com

Schiffer Publishing's titles are available at special discounts for bulk purchases for sales promotions or premiums. Special editions, including personalized covers, corporate imprints, and excerpts can be created in large quantities for special needs. For more information, contact the publisher.

CONTENTS

INTRODUCTION

Vintage hats. We love to look at them. We love to collect them. And, we love to wear them.

This book was put together as visual eye candy for the hat lover, as well as to provide an invaluable resource for costumers and collectors. It is presented chronologically spanning over seven decades and without commentary to influence the reader's own conclusions as to fads, fancies, construction, and dating. The hat styles are shown through original catalog scans with augmentation from a few magazine illustrations.

At the turn of the twentieth century catalogs gave American women the chance to see the latest styles and newest offerings in fashion. Although Sears, Roebuck and Co. and Montgomery Ward are the best known, there were many other companies, merchandisers, and store retailers who also had catalogs.

Some catalogs focused on a particular product, like the Fine Millinery Catalog, and some sold many types of garments and accessories, like Macy's. Even if the catalog specialized in shirtwaists, skirts, and coats, these items were shown fully accessorized with shoes, hats, gloves, or parasols, thus extending the marketing for hat and shoe companies. A woman could always find advertisements for specific clothing goods and catalogs to buy them in popular women's magazines of the day; all one had to do was ask to have a catalog or information sheet sent to their home.

Far left:
M. Philipsborn advertisement for their latest catalog. 1904 *Woman's Home Companion* magazine for November.

Left:
Macy's advertisement for their catalog. 1909 *Modern Priscilla* magazine for November.

Simpson Crawford Co. advertisement showing accessorized clothing and offering their free Fashion Book and Shopping Guide. 1910 *Modern Priscilla* magazine for September.

This made catalogs available to any miss or missus, whether she lived in a large city or on a remote farm. This gave every woman the opportunity to purchase the latest style offerings of their choosing. What was presented in picture form in the catalog was exactly what would be received in the mail after submitting an order and payment.

In the early years of the 1900s, hats were so important to a woman's wardrobe that ladies were encouraged to make millinery at home as a cottage industry, or at least to buy a basic hat and trim it themselves. Homemakers could start their own millinery business in their own house or out of a shop by purchasing hat lots at wholesale prices and reselling for a profit. Women's magazines presented "how-to" articles for updating and refurbishing last years' chapeau to keep up with the changing styles.

Chicago Mercantile Co. "Start a Millinery Business" advertisement. 1910 *Modern Priscilla* magazine for August.

Boston Store Chicago advertisement for popular clothing, but also showing the hat as accessory. 1910 *Modern Priscilla* magazine for May.

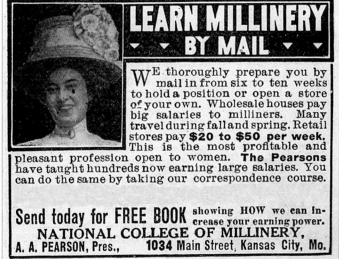

National College of Millinery "Learn Millinery by Mail" advertisement. 1910 *Modern Priscilla* magazine for October.

DECEMBER, 1907

"This new hat cost me 90c."

"What do you think of my new hat? It cost me just 90 cents. I changed the shape of my last Winter's hat—bought a remnant of beautiful red ribbon for 80 cents and a package of cardinal dye for 10 cents and dyed the old plume and it came out so fresh and new. I don't know what I would do without Diamond Dyes."

Mrs. J. W. Kelly, Boston, Mass.

Diamond Dyes Will Do It

Diamond Dyes advertisement for dyeing an old ostrich plume for a new look. 1907 *Pictoral Review* magazine.

$50 HAT for $17.75

The ostrich plume on this hat is our magnificent 26-inch hand-knotted willow. This plume elsewhere would cost $25.00. We sell for $12.75, a saving of 50%. How?—because we are the largest manufacturing importers of ostrich plumes in the world, selling direct to the consumer.

Get one of these plumes, tack it on a hat you can buy anywhere for $5, and you have a beautiful creation worth $50, which will excite the envy of your friends, for $17.75.

Advertisement to update or make an ordinary hat a beautiful creation with the addition of an ostrich plume. 1910 *Modern Priscilla* magazine for March.

Cawston Ostrich Feathers advertisement to buy new plumes or have your old ones refurbished. 1910 *Modern Priscilla* magazine for March.

The Edwardian period showed hats becoming bigger to be able to be worn over massive hairdos of the day. To augment their own locks and achieve big hair styles, human hair switches and braids were available by mail order and in stores. All a woman had to do was choose the hairstyle she wanted to achieve, pick the hairpiece to achieve it, and remit the order form, payment, and a sample of her hair for color matching. Her new hairpiece would later arrive in the mail and she was ready to sport her new hairdo.

Example of large hat, large hair. 1910 *Modern Priscilla* magazine for October.

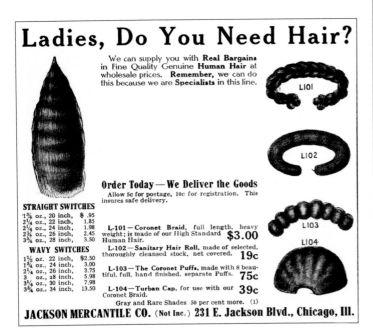

Jackson Mercantile advertisement for human hair pieces at wholesale prices. 1910 *Modern Priscilla* magazine for April.

Paris Fashion Co. human hair switches advertisement. 1910 *Modern Priscilla* magazine for January.

The 1920s brought about a time of extreme style changes with women bobbing their hair and wearing dresses well above the ankle. The ever-changing and most popular clothing styles of the day prompted hats and headwear to accessorize them.

The Depression of the 1930s brought times of desperation and want for many, while others continued to show their wealth by wearing many outfits throughout the day for various activities. An inexpensive new hat could perk up a tired old outfit, or a person of means could purchase a hat to match her every outfit. Hats were constructed with a tilt, or made to be worn tilted on the head.

The World War II years were a time of giving for the war effort and self-sacrifice. A new hat was easily obtained to renew the look of an old dress that had been hemmed shorter to keep up with the style of the day; a new pair of shoes was much harder to come by because of leather rationing. Oversized trimmings and upright feather quills adorned hats in eye-catching fashion. Statement hats to go with New Look styles after the War continued, while smaller hats began appearing on models and in magazines.

By the early 1950s, half-hats or wide headbands, or halo hats with a nose veil became common for daily wear. Feathers made a mighty comeback, but this time around they were small and plentiful enough to cover the entire hat instead of single ostrich plume, quill, or cockade of many decades earlier.

In the early 1960s, Jackie Kennedy brought the Pillbox hat to life. As the years passed, women started getting recognition as an equal gender, hippies replaced the beat generation, and hat popularity lessened to virtual non-existence as synthetic hair pieces and wigs became the extremely popular head covering of the day. Every female could instantly have the long tresses that were popular at the time, or always have perfectly

Selection of artificial hair wigs. 1972 Montgomery Ward catalog for Spring and Summer.

coiffed hair by simply slipping on a wig or pinning on a fall or braid. In only seven decades we seem to have come full circle with augmenting the hair and making the hat less important.

Today, in the 2010s, we still love hats and we still love catalog shopping, whether the catalog is received through the mail or quickly accessed on the internet.

A special note: Because of the age of the publications, there was yellowing, discoloration, and disintegration to many of the pages that were scanned for this book. These problems were corrected as much as possible. Some descriptions were left intact, but non-essential information was removed to better showcase the hats on the pages.

A wig can be a woman's best friend

Just as practical as they are beautiful. Always at hand and ready to wear—brush them a variety of ways. Made of Dynel® modacrylic that looks and feels like real hair. Hand wash in cold water, mild shampoo. Shake and hang up to dry—brush, the curl stays in. They never need setting . . . almost better than your own hair.

HOW TO ORDER ALL WIGS

IT'S EASY. . . just cut a hair sample 1½" long, 1½" wide—freshly shampooed or colored; or send us a picture showing the shade you'd like. We can match most shades perfectly. Send your order, along with hair sample or color picture

A "MY GIRL" is a luxurious wig from Moldo Tress. Young and free-spirited with straight bangs, long shoulder length hair. Machine sewn to a stretch net cap. For ordering and easy-care instructions, see above. Made in the Orient. Fits heads to 23". Storage box included.
25.00

B "IMPULSIVE" is one of Carousel's most versatile hairstyles. The illusory side part can be changed with a flick of a brush. Styled with the new, slightly longer tapered back. Machine sewn to a stretch net cap.
20.00

C "GIGI" is a short cut, casual hairstyle by Carousel. Fluff it up, or brush it close to the head—looks great either way. Machine sewn to a stretch net cap.
17.00

Hand-tied wig to comb any way you please

D "MAME" by Moldo Tress is a completely hand-tied and hand-ventilated wig. Every fiber is individually hand-tied to a very light stretch base so that you can comb it in any direction. Made in the Orient.
25.00

CHAPTER 1: 1872 TO 1919

DECEMBER 1872.

New York Fashions.

New York millinery fashion dictated a bonnet that was soft and puffy on top, then crushed and filled with roses, silk loops, or handmade lace. The rolled rims drooped most at the back of the ears. Trimmings generally massed to the back because the hair was worn so high. What is said for bonnets is equally applicable to hats except how they were worn on the head - bonnets further back and hats further forward. 1872 *Metropolitan* by E. Butterick & Co.

Clockwise from upper left: Velvetta fabric with straight brim, turned up back trimmed with two parrots and aigrettes; Velvetta with satin outlined edge, flaring on left and drooping over the hair in the back; Large hat with medium broad brim; Straight brim raised on one side over a bandeau, fish scale band and jetted coques in plume fashion; Gainesboro shape has five bias fold of contrasting colors around the crown and a broad front effect accented with two birds; Shepherdess shape with pheasant feather trim; hand-made dress shape that dips in front and back with crown drape, ostrich feathers, aigrettes, and rosettes. 1900 Sears, Roebuck and Co. catalog reprint.

Row (1) fancy straw, raised on left with fancy muslin roses; Wire frame straw trimmed with rosettes and plumes; Lace mohair in a Gainsborough style; (2) Lace braid in a Chipped style with rose trim; Straw over a wire frame with silk loops around brim and on crown; Dress style with raised sides and the crown covered in roses; (3) Short back Sailor trimmed with silk and lace; Turban raised on the left with folded braid crown and floral trim; Mushroom with droop brim and a rose and lace trim. 1902 Sears, Roebuck and Co. catalog reprint.

Examples of women's stylish ready to wear or to be trimmed hat styles including Sailors, Panamas, Walking, and Golfing hats. 1902 Sears, Roebuck and Co. catalog reprint.

Examples of hat trimmings such as plumes, ostrich tips, jet bead crowns, and hat pins. 1902 Sears, Roebuck and Co. catalog reprint.

Modernes Journal für deutsche Frauen

Aus dem Reich der diesjährigen Frühlingsmode.

Ein sehr schöner Stoff, der aus Seide und Wolle hergestellt wird, bildet eine beliebte Neuheit. Dieses neue Gewebe zeigt einen brillanten Glanz und hat Aehnlichkeit mit dem zarten Chiffonstoff. Die zarten Farben, in denen es meist erscheint, sind Silbergrau, Pfirsichblüte, Schilfgrün und Weiß. Abends beim Lampenlicht bringt der Stoff durch seinen glänzenden Schimmer einen ungewöhnlichen Effekt hervor.

Seide wird in diesem Frühjahr ungemein viel getragen, und man findet in den Seidenstoffen eine große Auswahl von feinen Geweben in reizenden Farben. Als Ausputz eleganter Kleider werden vielfach glänzende Besatzstücke gewählt. Gold, Silber, Stahl und Jet, künstliche glänzende Blumen, Sterne, Vögel, farbige Perlen, sowie Seidenspitzen, die besonders in alten spanischen Mustern erscheinen, alle diese Dinge werden zur Ausschmückung besserer Kleider verwendet.

Left to Right: German women in America are shown the latest hat style: a dressy veiled hat to be worn with a shirtwaist dress. 1900 *Modernes Journal fur Deutsche Frauen* (German).

A very new idea is the ready-to-adjust crown formed of an ostrich-plume. The feather is coiled to form a round crown, and then is carefully tacked to keep it firmly in shape. It makes an exceedingly attractive crown for a hat which has the brim either of velvet or fur. To be worn with plainer gowns there are crowns in the form of a great big rose, made of changeable velvet; the brim may be of kid, felt or breast-feathers.

Though the prices of imported winter hats are soaring higher and higher, yet there is no need, now that the adjustable crown has been thought of, for the girl of moderate means to despair, for it is easy to see that she can have many smart, different-looking hats for the same price that she would pay for one of the thirty-five-dollar creations.

HAT WITH REMOVABLE
FEATHER CROWN

Example of the new idea of ready-to-adjust crown formed of a coiled ostrich plume(s). 1904 *Woman's Home Companion Magazine* for November.

Oversized hat examples to wear with winter coats. 1902 Sears, Roebuck and Co. catalog reprint

Parisian Turban of velvet over a buckram frame and shirred crown. 1904 *Woman's Home Companion Magazine* for November.

Clockwise from upper left: Handmade imported hat with a drape of silk point d' esprit lace extending around to a fan shaped bow in the back; Turban faced with silk maline tuckings and edged with horsehair braid; Picture hat with silk medallion lace and a tam crown; Imported boat shape with silk maline tuckings and silk embroidered chiffon. 1904 Fine Millinery catalog, Spring & Summer.

TODD, SMITH & CO.

Correct Millinery

CHICAGO ILL.

No. **140B.** LIKE ABOVE CUT. A FANCY IMPORTED MODEL HAT. Entirely hand made over silk wire frame. Faced with pure White Silk Chiffon, laid on the new Shirred Tuck Effect. Very effective. The upper rim is trimmed with a drape of pure White Silk Point d' Esprit Lace extending around to the back, where it is caught in a fan shaped bow by an Imported Steel Ornament. The new Flattron crown is completely covered with Imported Roses in White shaded to Pink.

$8.95

No. **141B.** LIKE ABOVE CUT. AN IMPORTED HAND MADE TURBAN ON THE NEW CONTINENTAL SHAPE. This beautiful pattern is faced with tuckings of pure Silk White Maline. Edge of the rim is finished off with four rows of Imported White Horsehair Braid. Triangular crown covered with Imported Pink Roses. At the side is placed one of our long genuine White Ostrich Plumes.

$10.00

No. **142B.** LIKE ABOVE CUT. BEAUTIFUL IMPORTED PATTERN HAT IN THE NEW BOAT SHAPE. Entirely made over a silk wire frame. Faced with our very finest quality of Imported White Paroxiline Braid. The crown is made of very fine tuckings of pure Silk White Maline. A Scarf made of pure Silk Embroidered Chiffon encircles the edge in ruffled effect, ending at the back in Streamers caught up with an Imported Steel Ornament. The back is further ornamented with two Wheel Rosettes made of Imported Pink June Roses.

$12.00

No. **143B.** LIKE ABOVE CUT. A LADIES' PICTURE HAT MODELED AFTER ONE OF THE VERY FINEST OF IMPORTED PATTERNS. Entirely hand made over a silk wire frame of Imported Black Hair Braid. On the edge of the rim and crown are placed wide bands of Black Silk Medallion Lace. The Tam crown is encircled with Silk Velvet Forget-Me-Nots. The trimming at the side of this elegant pattern hat consists of two of our very finest Imported White Ostrich Feathers, made of hard, glossy fiber.

$15.00

No. 128B. LIKE ABOVE CUT. A LADIES' DRESS HAT, HAND MADE OVER A SILK WIRE FRAME. Faced with shirrings of Imported pure Silk Black Chiffon. Edged with seven rows of Imported Black Hair Braid, laid on in the new ruffled effect. The Pointed Crown is entirely formed of our finest quality of Imported Roses in a delicate shade of Pink. A drape of pure Silk Black Chantilly Lace fills in the rim, extending around to the back, where it ends in a fan shaped bow, held in place by an Imported Steel Ornament.

$4.95

No. 129B. LIKE ABOVE CUT. ONE OF OUR EXCLUSIVE IDEAS IN A LADIES' DRESS HAT. Entirely hand made over a silk wire frame. Faced with pure Silk Black tucked Chiffon, edged with narrow Gold Braid. The upper rim and Tam crown are formed of Imported Horse Hair Braid, edged with bright Jet Spangles. A wreath of Imported Roses and Foliage set off the front of the rim. At the side is placed a unique bow formed of pure Silk Japanese Silk with streamers extending over on to the crown and held in place by an Imported Buckle. The space between the flowers and the crown is filled in with pure Silk Black Chantilly Lace.

$4.95

No. 130B. LIKE ABOVE CUT. A PLEASING DESIGN IN THE NEW POINTED TURBAN EFFECT. Hand made over a silk wire frame. Faced with all Silk Light Brown Chiffon, laid on in folds. The heavy rolled rim and crown are completely covered with Imported Ivy Foliage and Berries. The space between the crown and rim is filled in with layers of Light Brown and Castor Chiffon. At the side is placed a Star Fish Rosette, made of Light Blue pure Silk Louisienne Ribbon with straps of the same extending over on to the bandeau.

$4.95

No. 131B. LIKE ABOVE CUT. A LADIES' OR MISSES' HAND MADE DRESS HAT WITH LARGE TAM CROWN. Entirely formed of a beautiful pattern of Imported pure Silk White Chantilly Lace laid on in close shirrings; the edge in ruffled effect. Trimming on the crown consists of a novel wreath of pure Silk Velvet Light Blue Forget-Me-Nots and bows of Imported Mousseline Taffeta Ribbon to match. Bandeau is

$4.95

Clockwise from upper left: Dress hat, handmade over a silk wire frame with pointed crown; Exclusive hat with tam crown, tucked chiffon, and gold braid; Handmade dress hat with large tam crown formed of shirred chantilly lace; Hat design with the new pointed turban effect and heavy rolled rim. 1904 Fine Millinery catalog, Spring & Summer.

TODD, SMITH & CO.

Correct Millinery

CHICAGO
ILL.

No. 116B. LIKE ABOVE CUT. A LADIES' DRESS HAT, ENTIRELY HAND MADE OVER A SILK WIRE FRAME. Upper and lower rims formed of accordion plaited, pure Silk Black Chiffon. Has a ruffle on the edge formed of numerous rows of Black imitation Hair Braid, edged with bright Spangled Jet. Entire crown is covered with Imported Pink Roses. Trimmed on the under facing with Flowers and Foliage to match.

$2.95

No. 117B. LIKE ABOVE CUT. LADIES' HAND MADE DRESS HAT. Faced with pure Silk tucked Black Chiffon, edged with numerous rows of Black Horse Hair Braid with ruffled edge, the crown being made of this same material and encircled with bands of pure Silk Black Taffeta Silk, ending at the back with Bow and Imported Cut Steel Buckle. A spray of Imported Pink Roses with Buds and Foliage ornament the side.

$2.95

No. 118B. LIKE ABOVE CUT. LADIES' HAND MADE DRESS TURBAN. Entirely made of Black pure Silk tucked Chiffon, edged with two rows of Imported Black Hair Braid, set off with Gold Cord. Crown is completely covered with Imported White Roses and Foliage. A Monture of these same Flowers and loops of Black Silk Velvet Ribbon ornament the side.

$2.95

No. 119B. LIKE ABOVE CUT. LADIES' HAND MADE BONNET. Made over a silk wire frame of imitation Horse Hair Braid. Trimmed on the Coronet with loops of this same material, edged with bright Jet Spangles. Set off with Cut Jet Ornament and Barbs of pure Silk Lace and two Pink Roses. Has Black Silk and Velvet Ties.

$2.95

Clockwise from upper left: Handmade dress hat of accordion plaited silk chiffon; Handmade dress hat with horse hair braid trim; Bonnet trimmed on the coronet with loops of imitation horsehair braid and jet spangles; Dress Turban of tucked chiffon and edged with imported hair braid and gold cording. 1904 Fine Millinery catalog, Spring & Summer.

Left to Right: Graduated tucked skirt over a tucked blouse with suspenders with the latest hat, gloves, and parasol; Circular fancy eton shown with a complimentary hat. 1905 Ladies World magazine for August.

Magazine illustration showing the latest ostrich plumed hat. 1909 *Modern Priscilla* magazine for January.

Example of larger hair and the oversized hat needed to fit it. 1909 *Modern Priscilla* magazine for November.

Scarf in Maltese Crochet and Knot Stitch

BY MAUD D. BURKS

Materials: Four skeins of cream white Shetland floss; one 10-cent ball of cream knitting silk; a 2¼-inch staple for the Maltese crochet; a small bone crochet hook.

THIS scarf is made of Maltese lace, joined together with knot-stitch. This new combination of stitches is called Coral Crochet. To make Maltese lace, tie the wool around the staple, with the prongs down. Holding it in the left hand, draw the wool under the loop on the staple and make 1 single crochet, keeping the work in centre of staple. Turn the staple towards you from right to left, keeping wool back of the left prong, and slipping the hook over the end of the staple with the stitch on it. Draw the wool through the loop on the left prong, and make 1 single crochet, and so on. When the staple is full slip off the work. If the required length is not made, leave a few loops of the lace on the staple, and proceed as before. Make up one skein of floss into Maltese lace. Beginning at the middle of this strip, catch 40 loops of lace together to make the scallop. Make one long knot-stitch and catch into three loops of lace on the other side, and so on back and forth to the other end of the strip, ending on the other side from the one on which you began. Now catch 40 loops together to form the scallop. This finishes the first strip. Make two more strips like this and join them together with knot-stitch caught back and forth into three loops of the lace, beginning on one side and ending on the other. Finish the edge with 5 chain stitches of silk caught into each three loops of the lace except at the ends, where the 5 chain is caught into each two loops of the lace. Use what is left of the fourth skein to make the rosettes. Edge with 5 chain of silk caught into two loops of lace, and draw up and sew in place. This scarf may be pinned to the hair under the rosettes, or tied under the chin with ribbon, or held in place by elastic, or left to hang loose, as preferred. See the Priscilla Crochet Book for other prices in Maltese crochet. Price, 25 cents.

HEAD SCARF IN MALTESE CROCHET AND KNOT STITCH

Maltese lace crochet cap and scarf. 1910 *Modern Priscilla* magazine for April.

A knitted hood. 1910 *Modern Priscilla* magazine for January.

Embroidered Hats

No. 10-5-30. ONE OF THE NEW SHAPES FOR LINGERIE HATS

No. 10-5-31. LINGERIE HAT IN FRENCH AND EYELET EMBROIDERY

Lingerie hat with round flat crown covered with embroidered linen or lawn to make at home. 1910 *Modern Priscilla* magazine for May.

A Scotch cap to knit. 1910 *Modern Priscilla* magazine for March.

Advertisement for Hinds Cream to be used before and after exposure to wind and sun. (And, the hat won't hurt, either.) 1910 *Modern Priscilla* magazine for September.

Good Sport
may be enjoyed without the
Torment of Sunburn

Rejuvenating Last Spring's Hat

NEAPOLITAN-WIDENED MUSHROOM WITH MALINE-COVERED WIRE CROWN

ROLLING BRIM BROWN CHIP WITH RIBBON-BUILT-UP CROWN

BLACK-NET-FACED LEGHORN WITH NET AND FLOWER CROWN

Examples of inexpensive "how-to's" for rejuvenating hats from the previous season. 1910 *Modern Priscilla* magazine for May.

Example of a hat to wear with a new soutache braided ensemble. 1910 *Modern Priscilla* magazine for October.

Example of feather popularity as hat trimming and as a boa. 1910 *Modern Priscilla* magazine for October.

New College
Coat Sweater

PRICE
$1.69

Smart Looking
Sweater Coat

PRICE
$1.95

Catalog advertisement showing
the latest sweaters and the hats
worn with them. 1910 *Modern
Priscilla* magazine for September.

An embroidered white linen shirt
waist suit accessorized with a large
Lingerie hat and parasol. 1910 *Modern
Priscilla* magazine for May.

Cool, Comfortable Mexican Palm Hat
For Man, Woman or Child   All Sizes   50c
Guaranteed genuine Mexican
hand woven from palm fibre; colored design woven in brim. Doesn't fray
or crack, and will outwear three ordinary straw hats.

Genuine
Panama $1

Special Introductory Bargain: **Imported Direct**
Same as a $10.00 Panama hat, but rather coarser weave. Weight
2 ounces. Very durable, and so flexible it can be shaped to any style
for man, woman or child. An ideal ladies' vacation hat. All sizes.

Mexican Palm hat and Genuine Panama. 1910 *Modern Priscilla*
magazine for May.

The New "Beach Hat" Sun-
bonnet has captivated the country.
Jaunty and chic, comfortable, ample
in size, it combines attractive style
and generous protection for sunny out-
of-doors days. Fits anyone, easily ad-
justed, light and cool; equally attractive for ladies and children. No ties or
frills to bother; made of fine quality
percale, in the newest shades. Just
to get acquainted, we will send
prepaid to any address for Twenty-five Cents.

Browne's

Ample Beach Hat Sunbonnet without ties. 1910 *Modern Priscilla*
magazine for April.

Latest dress fashions and the hats that were worn with them. 1911 The Mother's Magazine for June.

33 $2⁴⁹

15134 $2⁴⁹

32 $2⁴⁹

35 $1⁹⁸

36 $1⁹⁸

37 $2⁴⁹

(32) Woven Java straw with a silk velvet band; (33) Satin straw braid Mushroom; (34) Java straw with a high round crown and turned up brim in front; (35) Java straw Sailor with telescope crown and rolled edge; (36) Milan straw with striped silk scarf band; (37) Pressed hair braid with cockade of black silk Taffeta. 1913 National Cloak & Suit catalog for Spring & Summer.

TAILORED HATS FOR LADIES AND MISSES

32—You will be delighted with this jaunty and stylish Hat of fine hand-woven Java Straw, because it is graceful and becoming and very, very serviceable. Encircling the crown is a band of handsome silk velvet, finished with a tailored velvet bow, trimmed with silk fringe.

$2.49

33—Smart style and good materials are combined in this becoming Hat, and the price is only $2.49. It is one of the very newest mushroom styles and is made of Satin Straw Braid. A charming trimming is provided by silk messaline which encircles the crown in graceful folds and forms the smart wings at the left side.

$2.49

34—A $3.25 Hat for $2.49. You will be delighted with the individuality and smart style of this jaunty Hat of Java Straw faced with fine Neapolitan braid. The fashionable moderately high round crown and the brim which is smartly turned up in front, are extremely becoming and the trimming is very effective. Satin messaline ribbon encircles the crown in soft, graceful folds and terminates in a smart bow. NATURAL BLEACHED STRAW COLOR ONLY.

$2.49

35—Very smart, stylish and a bargain,—fashionable Java Straw Sailor Hat only $1.98. It has the favored telescope crown and rolled edge and is universally becoming. It is smartly trimmed with a broad band and flat bow of velvet ribbon. NATURAL BLEACHED STRAW COLOR ONLY

$1.98

36—Here is a real bargain. Only $1.98 for this attractive and serviceable Hat of Milan Straw. It is very stylish and becoming in shape, and the pretty striped silk scarf and straw buckle provide a smart trimming.

$1.98

37—Good style characterizes every line of this Tailored Hat of Pressed Hair Braid and Satin Straw Braid. It is one of the newest shapes and displays the fashionable front trimming in a jaunty cockade of black silk taffeta finished with bow of straw braid.

$2.49

(03) Satin straw braid Turban with draped crown and trimmed with ostrich and marabou fancy; (04) Silky hair braid with round crown and rolled brim with folds of messaline around the crown; (05) Straw Tam O'Shanter crown and narrow brim trimmed with roses; (06) Narrow brim Turban with crown covered in foliage; (07) Straw braid with brim rolled and turned up on left; (08) Silky hair braid with double-faced brim turned up at the side and finished with roses. 1913 National Cloak & Suit catalog for Spring & Summer.

03
$2.98

04
$2.98

05
$2.49

06
$2.98

07
$2.69

08
$2.49

03—A $3.75 Hat for $2.98—a stylish and becoming Turban of Satin Straw Braid. The graceful draped crown is of the newest shaping, while the brim is trimmed at the left side in two smart loops and a knot of the straw braid, and a beautiful ostrich and marabout fancy provides an attractive trimming.

$2.98

04—Very fashionable, serviceable and a bargain—a Hat of Silky Hair Braid. It has a becoming round crown, while the brim is slightly rolled all around in the newest style, and finished with a piping of rich velvet. Lustrous silk messaline is laid in graceful folds around the crown, and is used for the stylish large bow, which is finished with a handsome buckle of velvet and silk messaline.

$2.98

05—Only $2.49 for this fashionable Hat of Ratine and Silk straw with stylish Tam O'Shanter crown and a narrow brim slightly rolled up all around. Silk messaline ribbon encircles the crown, and pink roses and green foliage effectively trim the side.

$2.49

06—Very new—yes—and very beautiful and becoming and a remarkable value. This is one of the new Flowered Turbans. The crown is covered with handsome silk geraniums and rich foliage, while the narrow brim becomingly rolled all around, is covered with dainty crêpe chiffon laid in soft folds. A very pleasing new style note is the smart wing at the left side, which is also of crêpe chiffon.

$2.98

07—A real bargain—stylish Hat of Satin Straw Braid for only $2.69. It displays a round crown and medium brim, becomingly rolled and smartly turned up at the left side. Silk messaline ribbon encircles the crown and forms a beautiful bow at the left side, where pink roses provide an effective trimming.

$2.69

08—Here is style, beauty, becomingness and a saving of 75 cents. Silky Hair Braid is used for the top of the crown and the double-faced brim, which is smartly turned up at the side. Silk mousseline is draped gracefully around the crown and is finished at the left side with handsome tea roses and green foliage.

$2.49

38
$2.98

39
$3.98

40
$2.98

41
$2.98

42
$3.98

43
$2.98

TAILORED HATS FOR LADIES AND MISSES

38—A "NATIONAL" bargain—and a Hat that will delight you with its beauty, style and splendid quality and its very, very low price. It is made of Imported Fine Chip Straw and the round crown and very slightly rolling brim are universally becoming. Satin messaline ribbon is draped around the crown in folds and formed into loops in smart wing effect on each side.

$2.98

39—A more becoming Hat than this Tailored Model would be hard to find, and its very low price makes it a real bargain. It is made of handsome Satin Straw Braid and has the new style round crown and jaunty rolling brim. Silk messaline is used for the facing, the very stylish bow, and for the folds around the crown, which are uniquely strapped with bands of the straw braid.

$3.98

40—Smart and becoming Hat of Tagal Hemp Braid—stylish and serviceable and a bargain. The crown is of correct height and the drooping brim is very graceful and becoming. A draped scarf of corded silk is the effective trimming.

$2.98

41—This Tam O'Shanter Hat is greatly favored and always becoming. Silky Hair Braid is used for the stylish crown and turned-up brim, and a binding of black velvet, black satin messaline loops and a smart buckle provide the effective trimming.

$2.98

42—A saving of at least $1.00 on this Hat of Satin Straw Braid. The round crown is medium high, and the slightly rolling brim caught up at the left side and trimmed with a handsome wing, is very becoming. Velvet facing and velvet band.

$3.98

43—This handsome and becoming Hat is one of the newest and most serviceable models. It is made of Satin Straw Braid and has a stylish round crown and the rolling brim is faced with satin messaline. An effective trimming is provided by soft folds of satin messaline draped around the crown and finished with a smart messaline wing.

$2.98

(38) Imported chip straw with a round crown and slightly rolling brim; (39) Satin straw braid with round crown and rolling brim; (40) Tagal hemp braid with drooping brim and a draped scarf band; (41) Tam O'Shanter of silky hair braid; (42) Satin straw braid with medium high round crown and trimmed with a handsome wing; (43) Satin straw braid with soft folds of messaline draped around the crown finishing in a wing effect. 1913 National Cloak & Suit catalog for Spring & Summer

Seven Nobby, Stylish, Attractive Hats

(82) Nobby of French felt with rolling brim; (83) Telescope with rolling crown; (84) Imitation fur over buckram frame with rounded crown; (85) Turban over wire frame covered with folded taffeta; (86) Nobby Turban with felt wings; (87) Turban with small rolled brim and high crown; (88) Small rolling brim with folded moire silk around crown. 1913-14 W. & H. Walker catalog for Fall and Winter.

Seven Latest Styles in Hats

(61) Silk velvet over buckram frame with ostrich feathers; (62) Silk velvet with shirred silk and a large silk flower; (63) Silk paon velvet with 4" crown and imitation aigrette; (64) Silk plush looks like beaver with a rolling brim; (65) Mushroom with crown of shirred paon velvet; (66) Round crown with two rows of Bulgarian braid; (67) Silk velvet with rolling brim and a large willow plume. 1913-14 W. & H. Walker catalog for Fall and Winter.

Ladies' Trimmed Hats

(58) Round crown and rolling brim with 23" willow plume; (59) Roll shape bound with braid and trimmed in ostrich feathers; (60) Paon velvet with rolling brim and double ostrich plumes. 1913-14 W. & H. Walker catalog for Fall and Winter.

Ladies' Untrimmed Shapes

(89) Untrimmed velvet with round crown and roll brim; (90) Untrimmed velvet with high crown and roll brim; (91) Untrimmed velvet with round crown and large roll brim; (92) Untrimmed beaver felt with round crown and wide rolling brim; (93) Untrimmed beaver felt with round crown and wide rolling brim; (94) Untrimmed Nobby shape with rolling brim and round crown; (95) Untrimmed French felt is soft and pliable to be shaped; (96) Untrimmed French felt to be shaped; (97) Silk plush untrimmed with rolling brim. 1913-14 W. & H. Walker catalog for Fall and Winter.

Special Value Ladies' Hat Trimmings

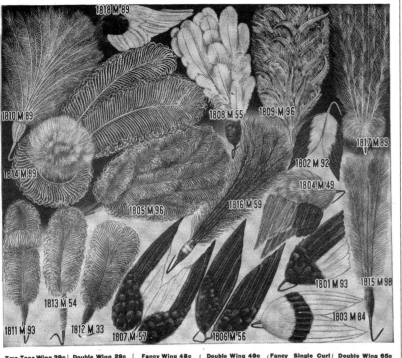

Two-Tone Wing 39c	Double Wing 29c	Fancy Wing 48c	Double Wing 49c	Fancy Single Curl Ostrich Trimming 69c	Double Wing 65c
This very pretty wing will make a beautiful trimming for any hat. Well made and rich appearing.	This will make a very pretty trimming for any hat. Is a double wing, well made and rich appearing.	This pretty wing is well made as illustrated. Is very solid and will not come apart.	The very pretty wing is well made as illustrated.	This is a very pretty hat trimming made of several single curl ostrich feathers. Very large and rich appearing.	This double wing is solidly made, is large and will make a very pretty hat trimming.
1801M93. Price.....39c Shipping wt., 1 oz.	1802M92. Price.....29c Shipping wt., 1 oz.	1803M84. Price.....48c Shipping wt., 2 oz.	1804M94. Price.....49c Shipping wt., 2 oz.	1805M96. Price.....69c Shipping wt., 2 oz.	1806M56. Price.....65c Shipping wt., 2 oz.
Double Wing 75c	**Fancy Trimming 55c**	**Fancy Feather 69c**	**Imitation Aigrette 98c**	**Fancy Ostrich Feathers 39c**	**Ostrich Hat Trimming 33c**
This pretty wing is made extra strong, and will give any hat a very rich appearance	One of the most popular feathers as illustrated. Very rich this season. Made of several curled feathers as illustrated.	This very pretty fancy feather is made of quills curled.	This trimming is made and has the appearance of an aigrette. Has several feathers.	This pretty hat trimming is made of two single curled ostrich feathers, in design, as illustrated.	This pretty trimming is made of two single ostrich feathers solidly curled in pretty design.
1807M57. Price.....75c Shipping wt., 2 oz.	1808M55. Price.....55c Shipping wt., 2 oz.	1809M96. Price.....69c Shipping wt., 2 oz.	1810M89. Price.....98c Shipping wt., 2 oz.	1811M93. Price.....39c Shipping wt., 2 oz.	1812M33. Price.....33c Shipping wt., 2 oz.
Fancy Feather 45c	**Fancy Feather 98c**	**Hat Trimming 89c**	**Fancy Feather 95c**	**Fancy Feather 98c**	**Double Wing 98c**
This pretty feather is made of two single curled ostrich feathers. Bound around with fancy trimming. A very rich appearing trimming for any hat.	This pretty feather is made of two single ostrich feathers curled in circle feather as shown with sprouts as illustrated.	This fancy feather is made and has the appearance of a genuine aigrette. Has five feathers.	This fancy feather is well made, and has the appearance of a genuine aigrette. Has six feathers.	This handsome feather is made and has the appearance of a sheaf of wheat design.	This is one of the prettiest double wings shown this season. Well made and will not blow out.
1813M54. e Price.....45c Shipping wt., 2 oz.	1814M89. Price.....98c Shipping wt., 2 oz.	1815M98. Price.....89c Shipping wt., 2 oz.	1816M59. Price.....95c Shipping wt., 2 oz.	1817M89. Price.....98c Shipping wt., 2 oz.	1818M89. Price.....98c Shipping wt., 2 oz.

Hat trimmings: (1801) Two-tone wing; (1802) Double wing; (1803) Fancy wing; (1804) Double wing; (1805) Fancy single curl ostrich; (1806) Double wing; (1807) Double wing; (1808) Multi-wing; (1809) Fancy feather of curled quills; (1810) Imitation aigrette; (1811) Curled ostrich feathers; (1812) Double ostrich feathers; (1813) Two curled ostrich feathers made to look like one; (1814) Two ostrich feathers curled in circle; (1815) Fancy feather look aigrette; (1816) Fancy feather look aigrette; (1817 Fancy feather has appearance of sheaf of wheat; (1818) Double wing. 1913-14 W. & H. Walker catalog for Fall and Winter.

The Fox Trot Cap

UNUSUALLY dainty is this little cap of net, lace, and embroidery. One might conclude from the illustration that it was somewhat difficult to make, but in fact it is very easy. The foundation is of net, eighteen inches square. This net is very fine and has small round meshes.

First work the embroidery design, and in order to do this the pattern must be stamped on paper. Baste the net over the paper, taking fine stitches around each section, so that it will be perfectly firm. A slight padding should be used to raise the design from the material, then work solid, taking the stitches through both paper and net. Either stem-stitch or outlining may be used for the stems, but naturally the stem-stitch gives a better effect. After the work is complete, carefully tear away the paper.

Now from corner to corner, crossing in the centre of the cap, sew a fine insertion. The net beneath may be cut

CAP OF NET AND LACE
By Harriet Webb

DESIGN No. 156-41. Design stamped on paper and wash blonde net, not stamped, 50 cents. Embroidery cotton, 7 cents extra. Valenciennes lace and insertion, 50 cents. Perforated pattern, 25 cents; transfer pattern, 10 cents.
Embroidery commenced, 75 cents additional.

away or not, just as one chooses. Even when cut away the seams will need no extra finish, as net will not ravel like other materials. Around the edge of the cap is sewed lace, matching the insertion. For a casing around the edge, use a narrow white ribbon, sewing it on the wrong side, following the head of the lace along the sides, and rounding off the corners, leaving the points beyond. Run a narrow ribbon in this casing and draw it up to fit the head. Wire the points so they will stand out as shown in the illustration.

Across the front is a fold of ribbon, either in white or a dainty color matching the gown. No other trimming is necessary, but an extra touch might be added by extending this around the back, or even by adding a dainty wreath or single flower. In any case, the trimming that is used should match the gown with which the cap is to be worn.

BACK VIEW OF CAP, SHOWING EMBROIDERY DESIGN

Dainty fox trot cap of net, lace and embroidery. 1915 *Home Needlework Magazine* for June.

Nippons for Sports and Garden Parties

Nippon style for sports and garden parties featuring stenciled birds and flowers. 1916 *Modern Priscilla* for July.

(56) Shirred messaline satin; (58) Straw brim with satin crown adorned with ostrich feathers; (60) Hemp Shepherdess with floral and bow trim; (62) Tricorne Turban with wired "ears"; (63) Four-cornered Turban on buckram frame with ostrich feather; (64) Blocked shape of Madagascar grass straw with wheat and daisy trim; (65) Hemp with large bow of bengaline silk; (66) Water proof maline brim with floral trim. 1916 Montgomery Ward catalog.

(68) Slightly sloping crown with rolled brim; (70) Soft top crown with ostrich plume trim; (72) Hemp blocked shape Sailor with telescope crown; (74) Draped crown Turban that rolls to the left; (76) Pyroxaline braid draped Turban with ostrich floss tips; (78) Left rolling brim with ostrich floss pompons and aigrettes; (80) Two rows of muslin roses around the crown; (81) Woven satin braid with ostrich plumes; (82) Turban on light-weight frame with muslin roses in a coronet effect. 1916 Montgomery Ward catalog.

(84) Cretonne and straw braid Sailor; (86) Straw braid with messaline silk crown and three 12" ostrich plumes; (88) Double brim hemp with muslin roses tucked between; (90) Blocked Sailor of hemp braid with Helmet crown; (92) Sloping crown and drooping brim of shirred maline; (94) Tricorne Turban with velvet ears on top of crown; (96) Two-brim effect of Cane Sear straw; (97) Leghorn straw with Helmet crown and slightly drooping brim; (98) Straw braid with wired messaline ears. 1916 Montgomery Ward catalog.

(16) Satin finished braid with wreath of Muslin flowers as band; (18) Pyroxaline braid on a light-weight frame with deep flange of messaline on brim; (20) Hemp braid with drooping brim and floral band; (22) Pyroxaline braid on a wire frame with shirred chiffon underfacing; (24) Shirred Chiffon brim and a pyroxaline braid crown on a wire frame; (26) Tricorn Turban with double folds on left; (28) Blocked hemp with ribbon band; (29) Shirred messaline crown softens the straw braid; (30) Pyroxaline braid Turban with ostrich and aigrettes. 1916 Montgomery Ward catalog.

(32) Tuscan straw braid with velvetta ribbon and muslin roses; (34) Pyroxaline braid on light-weight frame with two large ears on left; (36) Wired back bow and wreath of muslin roses; (38) Hemp crown with contrast satin brim; (40) Tricorn Turban with moire silk wired bow; (41) Corded effect side crown with a large muslin rose in front; (42) Framed Turban with rosettes; (43) Framed straw braid with 15" ostrich feather; (44) Framed Turban with burnt hackle fancy; (45) Leghorn straw with bands of wide and narrow velvet around crown; (46) Modified Tricorn Turban with silk draped crown; (47) Rose clusters on pyroxaline braid. 1916 Montgomery Ward catalog.

Aeroplane velvet Sailor with full crown extended to form a wing effect and elongated brim. 1916 *Modern Priscilla* magazine for October.

Advertisement for "New York Styles" from the Charles William Stores. 1916 *Modern Priscilla* magazine for February.

Wide brim hat to accessorize suit. 1916 Sears, Roebuck and Co. catalog.

Stylish striped hat, velour corduroy coat, and parasol. 1916 Sears, Roebuck and Co. catalog.

(40) Elaborately trimmed Chin-Chin; (45) Chin-Chin of glossy straw braid with crown band and bow; (50) Off-the-face of Milan hemp braid with a muslin rose covered front; (55) Off-the-face of lustrous chip straw braid with four flowers; (60) Taffeta draped crown and maline brim with roses; (65) Girls drooping brim hat with velvet ribbon and flowers; (70) Girls Poke of chip straw braid with trimming; (75) Glossy straw braid Chin-Chin; (80) Glossy straw braid woven into the popular chain body style. 1921 Sears, Roebuck and Co. catalog for Spring and Summer.

(85) Straw braid with muslin rose covered crown; (90) Off-the-face with two roses; (95) Piping straw braid Poke with floral wreath band; (100) Chin-Chin with silk brim; (105) Piping straw braid rolling brim with velvet daisies; (110) Chantilly lace brim contrasts taffeta crown and flange; (114) Crepe with embroidered brim edge and velvet flower cluster; (118) Off-the-face with wired maline brim which narrows in back; (120) Off-the-face with embroidered net brim accented with a tassel and straw braid crown. 1921 Sears, Roebuck and Co. catalog for Spring and Summer.

Clockwise from upper left: Batavia cloth and braid Sport hat; Distinctive double brim straw; taffeta silk wired bow on straw; Moderate sized Sailor; Large rolling brim Sailor; Off-the-face for dress or sport; Stunning four cornered hat; Moderate sized Sailor in pineapple braid; Satin off-the-face. Center: Small silk crepe Sailor with ribbon edged veil. 1921 Sears, Roebuck and Co catalog for Spring and Summer.

(45) Off-the-face with chip straw brim covered with flowers; (50) Hemp straw braid Poke with ribbon edged brim; (55) Glossy straw braid with drooping brim and floral band; (60) Batavia cloth draped Turban with aigrette; (65) Straw braid Chin-Chin with appliqued flowers; (70) Transparent braid Poke; (75) Off-the-face with single large appliqued poppy; (78) Straw braid Turban with trimmings; (85) Straw braid Chin-Chin with floral wreath on brim. 1921 Sears, Roebuck and Co. catalog for Spring and Summer.

(67) Diana Allen is adorable with velvet flowers and silk grapes wreath band; (73) Mabel Taliaferro wears a soft silk brim with a glossy braid crown; (77) Fine hair braid crown and maline brim with edging of braid; (82) Maline brim with braid edging over wire and crown accented with ostrich plumes; (87) Glossy braid brim and hackle feather crown; (93) Bow, underbrim and side of crown of soft braid with a silk crown; (97) Draped crown and soft brim with floral band; (03) Double layer accordion plaited crepe brim with a Tam O'Shanter crown. 1921 Sears, Roebuck and Co. catalog for Spring and Summer.

Cap with Sailor brim for outdoor wear. 1923 Montgomery Ward catalog for Spring and Summer.

Showing four styles of hexagon mesh veils with embroidered designs to be draped over or attached to a hatband. 1923 Montgomery Ward catalog for Spring and Summer.

Outdoor Cap with adjustable back shield. 1923 Montgomery Ward catalog for Spring and Summer.

(13) Poke brim with full dome shape crown; (17) Crepe de Chine scarf set; (21) Shirred gros de londre crown with a midway band of visca; (25) Six-piece crown with bound edge brim; (29) High crown Poke of gros de londre with bands of gold; (33) Mushroom with sprays of burnt peacock trimming in back; (37) Roll brim style of Crepe de Chine; (41) Six-pc tagal straw braid crown embroidered with silk and gold thread with droop brim; (45) Visca braid with applique flowers; (49) Poke with fan bow of moire ribbon across the back; (53) Poke with flower trim; (57) Upturned back with hair braid crown; (61) Mushroom with dome crown; (65) Poke with straight side high crown; (69) Cloche with watermelon crown; (73) Milan crown and scoop brim with bound edge; (77) Side roll with fan trim of burnt peacock around side and back. 1925 Montgomery Ward catalog for Spring and Summer.

(15) Striped crown with draped sides and upper brim; (19) Short back style with two color band; (23) Full fan of burnt peacock across the back; (29) Dome crown with bound edge brim; (31) Harmonizing color under brim and veil; (35) Cable brim and dented crown: (39) Plaited crepe crown with telescoped sides; (43) Novel crown with plaited brim; (47) Side roll brim and double ostrich pompon trim at side; (51) Roll brim shape with diagonal band across front; (55) Poke with front draped crown and Visor brim; (59) Dome crown draped to each side with harmonizing under brim: (63) Close-stitched hemp and pliable; (67) Poke with embroidered veil; (71) Sides of alternate telescoped rows of gros de londre and plisse' silk crepe; (75) Crown with telescoped sides and outer brim of plaited crepe; (79) Crown draped to each side over a wide draped band of harmonizing color; (83) Drooping brim with fancy striped visca on crown. 1925 Montgomery Ward catalog for Spring and Summer.

(09) Piping straw with wide flange of hair braid around the brim; (13) Poke brim for the new bobbed hair style; (17) Off-the-face shape with ruffled flange on brim; (21) Snug-fitting Radio hemp with a dainty brim; (25) Tricorne brim and roomy crown for matrons; (29) Milan hemp with a gros de londre brim; (33) Watermelon crown with piped tinsel braid; (35) Off-the-face with hair braid flange edged brim; (39) Poke with plaited crown; (43) Visca cloth with bird's head and wide ostrich flue pad; (47) For matrons with a pin through front of crown; (51) Roll brim style with self trim; (55) Satin with high directoire crown; (59) Drooped front brim with four color draped band; (63) Patent milan with creased dome crown and off-the-face brim; (67) Tricorne with ostrich quill across the back; (71) Off-the-face brim and high crown; (75) Off-the-face style with telescoped side of Candy Cloth. 1925 Montgomery Ward catalog for Spring and Summer.

(41) Large dressy style with short back brim; (45) Round crown and narrow Tricorne brim for matrons; (49) Paris high crown style; (53) Small visor brim with trim at the face; (57) Mushroom shape with hairbraid flange extending over the underbrim: (61) French Turban of gros de londre and moire ribbon; (65) Birdnest straw with dainty roll brim; (69) Large brim style with sides and underbrim of harmonizing color; (73) Roll brim with dome crown piped from front to back with gathers; (77) Dome crown rising from a narrow brim: (81) Crown draped on the bias in a semi-tam effect; (85) Plaited brim with rosette trim; (89) Chin shape has roll brim all around; (93) Large brim with underbrim and brim edge of lustrous cloth; (97) Copy of Reboux Paris in fancy hemp with novel bow; (01) Directoire crown with triangle flange on either side; (05) Braided all around the brim in harmonizing color; (09) Straight sided satin crown. 1925 Montgomery Ward catalog for Spring and Summer.

(37) High crown in candee cloth; (41) Crepe crown with hemp brim; (45) Snug-fitting style with folded brim for the Parisian effect; (49) Poke with flut d crepe crown and upper brim; (53) Fine hairbraid in a full side draped crown; (57) Radio hemp with a smart roll brim; (61) Hemp with folded band and back bow of moire ribbon; (65) Six-piece crown trimmed with twisted two-color draped band and ostrich pompon; (69) High cuff corded brim with tinsel braid piping on crown with six-piece effect; (73) Drooping brim with sharp flange with tinsel braid piping; (77) Creased crown, telescoped band, and mushroom brim of overlapping rows of hairbraid; (81) Draped crown and cuff brim; (85) Off-the-face hairbraid crown and underbrim; (89) Six-piece crown of visca cloth; (93) gros de londre draped crown and visca upper brim in harmonizing colors; (97) Tricorne with piped telescope crown; (01) Six-piece crown with visor brim; (05) Plaited visca cloth with roll brim. 1925 Montgomery Ward catalog for Spring and Summer.

Young woman sportily dressed to show her Fourth of July spirit. 1927 *The Town Crier, The Wichita (KS) Beacon* newspaper for July 3.

Sporty ski outfits accessorized with headwear and scarves. 1927 *People's Popular* magazine.

Casual women's sweater with the perfect hat. 1927 Montgomery Ward Book No. 4 sale catalog.

(A) Sporty felt with soft crown; (B) Poke brim turned up in back; (C) Felt with creased crown and cut-outs in front woven with contrasting ribbon; (D) Felt Poke with striped ribbon band; (E) Felt New York with contrast band; (F) Creased crown felt Tam with rolled brim; (G) Narrow brim felt with creased high back; (H) Felt with ripple brim and creased crown; (J) Narrow brim felt with stitched and creased crown; (K) Nobby felt with creased crown and front and back roll brim; (L) Felt with creased crown and turned up back; (M) Poke with gigolo crown. 1927 National Cloak and Suit catalog for Spring and Summer.

Row (1) Poke of timbo hemp; up-turned brim rolled higher in front and back; Faille and metallic embossed cotton duvetyn in a draped Tam; Pyroxaline braid crown and sateen brim Poke; (2) Milan hemp with flexible brim; Poke with braid crown and taffeta brim; (3) Poke with ostrich trim; Straw braid alternates with embroidered crepe crown; Poke with floral cluster; Narrow rolled brim and coronet style front with pin ornament. 1927 National Cloak and Suit catalog for Spring and Summer.

(79) Poke of visca straw braid with ruffled flange; (82) Taffeta with rolled brim and embroidery; (84) Poke of semi-transparent pyroxaline braid; (86) Tam effect Poke with stitched brim; (87) Poke of pyroxaline braid and draped taffeta; (90) Ripple brim straw braid; (91) Transparent braid frill on a close-fitting Poke; (94) Parisian Tam of crocheted straw braid; (97) Draped Turban of imitation horsehair; (98) Semi-transparent braid with large brim rolled in back. 1927 National Cloak and Suit catalog for Spring and Summer.

(13) Novelty braid Poke with contrasting color brim; (14) Semi-transparent braid with roll brim; (16) Faille close-fitting Poke; (17) New York Tam of taffeta; (18) Transparent hair braid with creased crown and close brim; (19) Faille ripple brim with draped crown embroidered in straw braid; (20) Wide brim of semi-transparent braid; (21) Poke of canton crepe with draped flange; (22) Straw with narrow brim. 1927 National Cloak and Suit catalog for Spring and Summer.

(10) Poke with fruit trimming; (11) Off-the-face straw with celluloid ornament; (12) Straw Poke with floral spray; (13) Suede-finished cotton Poke; (14) Rolling brim Sailor; (15) Straw braid Poke with sateen crown and wide band; (16) Suede-finished cotton Poke with large flower; (25) Rhinestone ornaments; (93) Hat insert for a perfect fit; (Center top) Natty soft felt adjustable to any shape. 1927 National Cloak and Suit catalog for Spring and Summer.

(A) Birdsnest hemp braid with flowerlets; (B) Visca crochet braid with pyroxylin hair braid brim that sweeps the brow; (C) Swiss ajour hair braid and chantilly lace; (D) Visca braid with intricate brim; (E) Embroidered net crown; (F) Poke of pyroxylin hair braid and chantilly lace; (G) Picture of ajour braid with flange of birdsnest hamp braid; (H) Pyroxylin hair braid embroidered with fine visca thread; (J) Cut-away brim manipulated coronet-wise with pleated ribbon accent. 1927 Chicago Mail Order catalog.

(A) Perle visca hemp body with organdie roses; (B) Close-fitting bonnet-like Turban; (C) Silk georgette over vellocloth; (D) Poke with half wheels of rayon chapeau satin of the ears; (E) Flare brim dips its sides; (F) Pleated fan effects over each ear; (G) Side creased Poke; (H) Poke with draped band of metallic embroidered lace; (J) Poke of transparent ajour braid; (K) Picture hat of alternating birds nest hemp and fancy hemp braids; (L) Creased brim of birdsnest hemp braid. 1927 Chicago Mail Order catalog.

(A) Copy of Jean Patou hat with diamond ribbon appliques; (B) Scalloped embroidered lace crown with bonnet like brim; (C) Highbrow effect that dips low at both sides; (C, lower right inset) Hemp braid with dipped side brim; (D) Open weave Swiss straw braid with ribbon band; (E) Fancy hemp braid with a short back and wide brim. 1927 Chicago Mail Order catalog.

(F) Pleated and tucked to hug the face with long sides; (G) Bangkok weave Toyo with creased brim; (H) Lacy hemp braid with single folded side; (J) Helmet of silk georgette over a felt foundation; (K) One side folds like an Eastern Turban while the other has bengaline ribbon bows; (L) Turban of Skinners crepe back satin with hand painted flowers. 1927 Chicago Mail Order catalog.

Clockwise from upper right: Skull cap with felt appliques for misses; Eyebrow style of soft felt for larger sizes; Velvet with dainty mother of pearl flowers on satin rosettes for matrons; Creased crown with grosgrain band for children; Turban of shirred rayon faille with nose veil for women. 1928-29 Sears, Roebuck and Co. catalog for Fall and Winter.

Row (1) Two-piece felt; Felt with beaded rosette; Clara Bow Tam with embroidered design across front and encircling top of crown; Clara Bow Eyebrow style with jaunty brim; (2) Lyons velvet with transparent brim of metallic thread; Close-fitting shape of felt with rayon lining; Metallic embroidered crown with pleated brim; Eyebrow style with contrasting flower; (3) Velvet with baronet satin rolled brim; Varicolored embroidery on felt; Close-fitting style with slashed crown; Silk velvet Turban with wide band of satinette feathers. 1928-29 Sears, Roebuck and Co. catalog for Fall and Winter.

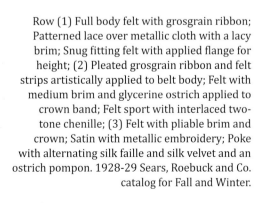

Row (1) Full body felt with grosgrain ribbon; Patterned lace over metallic cloth with a lacy brim; Snug fitting felt with applied flange for height; (2) Pleated grosgrain ribbon and felt strips artistically applied to belt body; Felt with medium brim and glycerine ostrich applied to crown band; Felt sport with interlaced two-tone chenille; (3) Felt with pliable brim and crown; Satin with metallic embroidery; Poke with alternating silk faille and silk velvet and an ostrich pompon. 1928-29 Sears, Roebuck and Co. catalog for Fall and Winter.

Row (1) Lovely Lady style felt with ostrich tassel; Crushable of belting ribbon; (2) Draped velvet with novelty cut brim; Felt Turban with felt trimming strips; Close-fitting felt with pleated wide crown band; (3) Felt with appliqued velvet ribbon band; Bengaline Turban with metallic embroidery; Felt with tucked crown and turned up brim; Felt with grosgrain ribbon trim set with brilliants. 1928-29 Sears, Roebuck and Co. catalog for Fall and Winter.

Row (1) Soft brim with metallic ribbon band; Felt with hand-tailored grape motifs; Close-fitting felt with felt rose (2) Felt with decorative stitching on crown; Fur velour with up or down brim; Soft brim felt with hand lacing in crown; (3) Sport hat of silk faced velvet; Eyebrow line brim with novelty braid inserted in crown; Felt with tucked crown; Gadabout of felt with ribbon trim. 1928-29 Sears, Roebuck and Co. catalog for Fall and Winter.

Clockwise from upper left: Azure straw braid with tuck crease crown, winsome brim and cutaway back; Swiss hair and pedaline straw braid sewed row on row with off-the-face brim and cutaway back; Irregular Eyebrow brim cut away at back and a nose veil; Azure straw braid with droop brim shortened toward the back; Vagabond felt; Ear-tab Cloche of rock hemp straw braid; Skull-cap Turban with nose veil; Embroidered hair braid in crochet effect with swirl cuff brim; Wide-brim sunshady of hemp straw sewed row on row. 1928 Montgomery Ward August 31 sale catalog.

Casual hats with sporty knickers; dressier hat for winter wear. 1928 Montgomery Ward August 31 sale catalog.

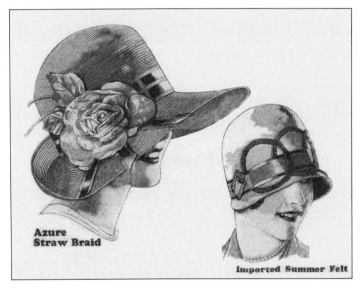

(Left) Straw braid with fashionable droop brim; (right) Soft Summer weight felt with pliable short brim.

Caps to wear with everyday clothing. 1929 Montgomery Ward sale catalog.

Knit cap to match a sweater. 1929 Montgomery Ward sale catalog.

Clockwise from upper left: Felt off-the-face with side curl bow; Wide brim summer braid; Tailored felt with slashed brim at side; Wool felt crusher. 1929 Montgomery Ward Book 1 sale catalog.

Row (1) Brow bearing with tuck across crown; Fedora with crown crease; (2) Up in the back, down over the eye line brim; "Visor" effect Beret; Breton Sailor with rolled brim; Sailor with swirling line crown tucking. 1929 Montgomery Ward catalog.

Row (1) Turban with embroidered mesh veil; Sailor with feather band; Mannish with deep tuck in the crown; Side roll brim; (2) Breton Sailor sweeps of the face; "Rough Rider" side roll brim; (3) Turban with tucked edge and veil; Cuff brimmed Tricorne; Turban with tucked and shirred side pieces; Sporty style with upturned brim; Knit hat for sportswear. 1929 Montgomery Ward catalog.

Clockwise from upper left: Center crease crown worn at rakish tilt; Off-the-face halo with quill; Turban with feather pads; Dipped brim with feather trim; Sporty mannish style; Dip brim with veil; "Shovel" brim with leather band and bow; Low crown with stitched brim; Pleated visor brim. 1929 Montgomery Ward catalog.

Clockwise from upper left: Beret with visor; Tilted Tam Beret; Breton Sailor; Stitched brim comes to a point in front; Mannish style with stitched brim; Four-Way Breton Sailor; Shallow crown Sailor; Breton Sailor with artificial leather bow; Creased crown with feather trim; Dipped brim with embroidered mesh veil; Halo Beret; Beret with feather trim. 1929 Montgomery Ward catalog.

Left half, top to bottom: All wool French Beret; Formal Beret; Brimmed knit in two-tone; "Gob" hat for sports; "Wing topped" turban; Knock-about Beret.
Right half, top to bottom: Wide wale corduroy with stitched brim; Narrow wale corduroy with scoop brim; Sailor of cotton suede cloth; Up in back, down over the eyes in cotton suede cloth; Cotton knit zig-zag turban and matching ascot scarf; Wide wale corduroy Beret and matching ascot scarf. 1929 Montgomery Ward catalog.

Clockwise from upper left: Close-fitting Knock-about of tinseled felt; Parisian Skull hat; Metallic brocade Helmet; Soleil-finish crushable wool felt with off-the-face brim and low hooded back; Off-the-face with fashion band to catch the brim; Poke with front droop brim, creased crown, and turned up back; Close-fitting Helmet of crushable faille with tinseled soutache trim; Wing effect is a combination of Skull and off-the-face lines. 1930 Montgomery Ward February 28 sale catalog.

Paris Styled Hats at Bargain Prices

True Copies of Lovely Paris Models
At a Saving of One-Half!

$1.98
Bargain Price

Clearance Prices on Stunning Velvets!

$1.29

Examples of clearance styles of Paris Models or embroidered velvet. No style may be chosen at clearance price. 1930 Montgomery Ward Book 1 sale catalog.

Authentic Styles—Prices Cut!

$1.29

Were $1.98 to $2.98

Copies of Imports— Surprising Values!

512 H 152—Every model in this group represents late Hat designs, worked out in soft wool felt. All styles are similar to the ones shown—any of the group is sure to please you. But there are only a few of each, so speed your order—and **don't forget to state second and even third color choice.**

$1.98

Was $2.98

Price Cut ⅓!

512 H 232—Price cut while in the height of style! Youthful Drape Brim favorite in beautifully soft All-Wool felt. To avoid disappointment get your order in at once. Will fit

Examples of clearance styles as Copies of Imports. No style may be chosen at clearance price. Far right: All wool felt with drape brim. 1930 Montgomery Ward Book 1 sale catalog.

Clockwise from upper left center: Wool felt with grosgrain trim; Felt Sports Hat; Pin front and bow back; Perforated Tam; Matron's hat in wool felt; Wool and silk stripe knit Beret; Center: Slashed turn-back brim. 1930 Montgomery Ward Book 6 sale catalog.

Examples of clearance styles in wool felts, silk-faced velvets or chenilles, straws and hairbraids, or various other materials with no choice of style at clearance prices. 1930 Montgomery Ward Unload sale catalog.

Clockwise from upper left: Parisian replica with the brim slashed at either side and brought up across the front of the crown; crushable hat with side flare brim; Wool felt with slashed and draped brim; close-fitting hat with slashed brim and a feather pad; hat with turn back brim, folds, and drapes; hat with molded crown, stitched brim, and tassel ornament; Beret with headband of grosgrain ribbon. 1930 National Bellas Hess catalog.

Clockwise from upper left: Close-fitting velvet hat with tucked tam crown; Tweed Beret Tam; Draped Turban; Cloche with embroidered tinsel braid; Soft felt with "angel" brim, velvet "angel" brim and shallow crown; Knitted Hindu Turban; Brushed wool Beret; Knit wool Turban; Silk-faced velvet with satin plaited ribbon; Wool felt in extra large size. Center: Cloche with hand made flower. 1930 National Bellas Hess catalog.

Row (1) Wool felt Bicorn; Rolled back brim; (2) "Baby Bonnet"; Sweep brim; Satin folded crown; (3) Velvet appliques; Brim longer on one side; Beret with tam crown; Ribbon back bow with three loops; (4) "Angel Face" brim; Flare brim; Brow revealing hat; "Baby Bonnet". 1930 National Bellas Hess catalog.

Row (1) Beret; Manipulated fabric for off-the-face; Raised brim on right dips to low scoop on left; Flared brim; (2) Shallow slashed crown; (3) Upward curving brim; Flare brim with back bow; Grosgrain ribbon cockade and novelty pin; (4) Drooping ostrich feather tassel; Appliqued crown; Fur felt Tam; Plaited cockades on either side of crown. 1930 National Bellas Hess.

Row (1) Rolled brim for off-the-face; "Bell" trim; (2) Back rolled brim; rolled brim; Vagabond style with applique; (3) "Pakaway" to be worn three different ways; (4) "Angel Face" brim turned up in back; Pins and clips for hats or dresses; Flared brim. 1930 National Bellas Hess catalog.

Four categories of clearance hats: wool felts, velvets, straws and hairbraids, chenilles. 1930 Montgomery Ward Unloading Sale catalog.

Latest Style

"WATTEAU"

$1.00

Hemp Braid and Flowers
A Breath-Taking Value!

A new low rounded crown, the tilting brim edged with soft hair flange, and coquettish flowers are all the very newest. Really exceptional quality for this price.

Low rounded crown and tilting brim edged with soft hair flange. 1931 Montgomery Ward Book 3 sale catalog.

Clockwise from upper left: Big floppy hat of lacy hemp straw; Flat crepe with two-tone halo; Toyo Panama Sailor; Eight ligne hair braid trimmed with ribbon; Lacy hemp braid with grosgrain ribbon for the matron; Doughboy crown with flattering brim. 1931 Montgomery Ward Book 3 sale catalog.

The Very Newest Styles

DIRECT from NEW YORK

To Be Pretty In

Summer just isn't summer without a big floppy hat to wear with organdies and dimities and garden-party frocks! But whoever dreamed of finding exactly the one you want for a dollar? You'll love the provocative droop of the lacy hemp straw brim and the chic of its splashing novelty ribbon bow.

Put on a Paris "Halo"

Flat Crepe with two tone halo.

Toyo Panama

A favorite with Paris, here is a fetching new Toyo Panama sailor, that's really not at all like the sailors of other years for it has the new up-tilt and the cunning shallow crown that say "here comes 1931." Its gay Roman striped grosgrain band lends just the right note of color chic. And amazing—it's only a dollar!

Watteau a la 1931

For the Smart Matron

Light weight transparent hair braid. Doughboy crown with flattering brim. Novelty flower trim.

Lacey hemp braid with grosgrain ribbon.

Sheer Loveliness in Hair Braid

If it's sheer, you know it's smart! Eight ligne hair braid combined with novelty hair and stunningly trimmed with lustrous ribbon of extra fine quality.

(A) Angora long nap Beret (B) Poke brimmed with lace (C) Lacy transparent cellophane guimpe (D) Transparent pyroxylin and fancy hair braid (E) Wrap around Turban (F) Beret and scarf set (G) Sunburst Beret (H) "Angel Face" of transparent pyroxylin hair braid and hemp straw (K) Sporty rolled brim (L) Cushion brimmed of rock hemp straw (M) Fan shaped plaited motif (N) Brim is flared, folded and trimmed (P) "Angel Face" for young girls (R) Poke shape for young girls (S) Vagabond style of two-tone tuscanette straw for young girls. 1931 National Bellas Hess catalog.

(A) Bicorne of viscas straw (B) "Off-the-face" rolled brim (C) Close-fitting style of bengaline (D) Off-the-face with balibuntl light weight straw (E) Transparent hat with brim of Swiss ajour (F) Wear it turned up, or wear it turned down (G) Rayon crepe crown with folded brim (H) Bicorn with unusual line at the forehead of visca straw (K) Long back and off the forehead line (L) Flare brimmed of rock hemp straw (M) Transparent pyroxylin hair braid crown (N) Unusual Bicorn style (P) Softly creased brim and plaited motif (R) Closely fitted of visca straw braid. 1931 National Bellas Hess catalog.

Row (1) Pedaline Straw Braid with "angel face" brim and ostrich feather; Visca straw with rolled brim; Bicorne with baku weave brim; (2) Intricately draped and folded pedaline straw braid; Off-the-face with patent leather ornament; Transparent pyroxylin hair braid with flare brim; (3) Sheer, fancy weave Bicorne; Transparent pedaline straw braid Bicorne; Two-tone cellophane and visca straw braid with rolled brim; Closely fitted Tam; (4) Cellophane and visca straw braid with long creased side and turned-up back; Conservative style of transparent fancy weave. 1931 National Bellas Hess catalog.

Row (1) Hemp straw cloche; Pedaline straw braid in balibuntl weave Bicorne; Bicorne with ostrich tip trim; Crushable Turban; (2) Baku weave Bicorne; Scalloped brim Bicorne; Baku weave Bicorne with self bow; (3) Transparent spider web weave Bicorne with self bow; Shiny pedaline straw braid and cloth with rhinestone ornament; Creased straw in spider web weave. 1931 National Bellas Hess catalog.

Row (1) copy of Marie Alphonsine drooping brim on snugly fitted crown; copy of French designer Rose Descat "halo" brim set high on the crown; copy of Molyneux roll brim creation; (2) copy of Agnes close-fitting, off the forehead crown; copy of Caroline Reboux transparent of fine net all-over embroidery; copy of V. Suzanne Talbot balibuntl weave Bicorne with ostrich tassel. 1931 National Bellas Hess catalog.

(A) Pirate with turned-back brim that is cut away from the crown and pleated at one side; (B) Pedaline braid with scalloped brim; (C) Bicorne of baku patterned braid; (D) Panama weave Toyo; (E) Pirate with the look of a kerchief being tied about the head; (F) Flowing brim Picture. 1931 Chicago Mail Order catalog

(A) Transparent Pyroxylin hairlike braid with bandeau brim; (B) Brim follows face contour, tucked, turned under, and tacked at each side; (C) Pedaline braid with a brim that turns back and then rolls forward; (D) Halo with attached pearl simulating ear-drops; (E) Viscalacque weave with Bicorn brim; (F) Picture to flatter the eyes. 1931 Chicago Mail Order catalog.

(F) Bow trimmed Frenchy; (G) Halo with a pirate brim, creased and turned back; (H) Spanish bandeau Sailor of baku patterned braid; (K) Silk and rayon faille taffeta Bicorne; (L) Lacy hemp braid with bandeau brim. 1931 Chicago Mail Order catalog.

(A) Cir'e pyroxylin hair-like braid with swanky bow; (B) Betty Jane Poke with brim inserts; (C) Crochet weave hemp braid with a brim that circles low on one side and curls up on the other; (D) Shallow crown with upturned back; (E) Pyroxylin braid with coronet and embroidered net applique; (F) Picture with folded brim. 1931 Chicago Mail Order catalog.

(G) Forehead banded, shoulder dipping lines of Egyptian headgear; (H) Cushioned Halo brim with a cutaway back; (J) Tricorne with feather trim; (K) Lacy hemp braid with Split Back brim; (L) Visca cloth Tam with velvet bandeau; (M) Poke of gingham-patterned braid. 1931 Chicago Mail Order catalog.

YOUR CHOICE
49¢

YOUR CHOICE
69¢
Sold up to $1.98

Special Close-Out Prices

(A) Every hat in this group represents a late style in Hair braids, rayon viscas, all over embroidered net pedaline straw; bangkok weave braid tweeded hairbraid, and all over lace. Flower, ribbon, quill or flower and lace trimmed.

(B) Extra Special Values

Designs similar to one shown—Hair braids, rayons, cellophane, straw, viscas, belting ribbon, baku braid, all over embroidery cloth. Handsomely trimmed with flowers, ribbons, ornaments and some with veils.

(C) Stupendous Bargains

A splendid group of Rayon viscas, all over embroidered nets, pedaline straws, fancy braids and all over laces. Smart flower, ribbon, etc. trimmings.

(D) Priced to Sell Out!

A group of charming styles similar to the one shown. Visca braids and straws, hair braids, straw braids, rayon satins with cellophane, all over embroidery, with gay touches of flowers, ribbon, quills, etc.

(E) Now! Big Savings

Summer charms in this group of "Picture" type hats. So popular and so low priced too. There are Hair braids, lacy straws, novelty straw braids, etc. Ribbon, flower or sash trim.

In this group are Hair braids, straw, Hair and straw combinations, Hemp body, embroidered rayons and georgettes. Some are feather trimmed, others ribbon or flower trimmed, etc.

Group of Hair braids, hair and straw combinations, hemp, embroidered rayon and georgettes and all straw. Trimmed with flowers, ribbon, feathers or embroidery.

Each a fetching style with tricky brims similar to one shown above. Some are all felt others felt and rayon satin combination. Smart trimmings such as flowers or ornaments.

Representative examples of clearance hats in various fabrics, styles, and colors. If purchased, buyer would be sent a similar style. 1932 Montgomery Ward Book 2A sale catalog.

More representative examples of clearance hats in various fabrics, styles, and colors. If purchased, buyer would be sent a similar style. 1932 Montgomery Ward Book 2A sale catalog.

Example of huge Picture hat popular in the 1930s. 1931 *Needlecraft, The Magazine of Home Arts* for September.

ANY OF THESE HATS
VALUES up to $2.00

YOUR CHOICE Sold up to $2.00
59¢

Big Close-Out Values

(F) Included in this lot are hair braids, lustrous rayons, cellophane, straw viscas, belting ribbon, baku braids or all over embroidery. Trimmed with ribbon, flowers, etc.

Act Quickly—Buy Now!

(G) Materials in this group are hair braids, lacy straws, novelty straw-braids, rough and plain straws, tuscan with hair. Trimmed with ribbon, etc.

Order Several and Save!

(H) Group of straw, hair and visca braids, crochet straw viscas, rayon satin with cellophane, all over embroidery. Trimmed with hair braid and feathers, novelties, ribbon, etc.

Smart—Snappy Styles

(J) Triumphs in style, quality and value! Included in this group are charming styles in straw and hairbraids, similar to one pictured. Trimmings are flowers, ribbon, fancy ornaments and smart quills.

Bargain Priced!

(K) It seems nothing short of unbelievable to get such quality for 49¢. In this group are Toyo weave Panamas with smart drooping brims. Each attractively trimmed with ribbon or harmonizing sashes.

A smart assortment of straw braids, hair braids or rayon taffeta failles. Designed especially for stylish young matrons. Some have ribbon trimming and others have flowers or fancy ornaments. Only a limited number left—order at once—you'll be delighted.

Charming styles for matrons who look for a dash of modernity and conservativeness. In this group are strawbraids, rayon taffeta failles and hairbraids. Each attractively trimmed with ribbon, flowers and fancy ornaments. Stocks are limited—Order now!

Semi-kepi Military style of corded knitted rayon fabric. 1933 Chicago Mail Order catalog.

Left to right: Dip brim wool felt with veil; Rabbit and wool knit with back bunny ears and veil. 1933 Chicago Mail Order catalog.

Evening and daywear fashions and the hat styles that go with them. Lower left hat is a veiled Dip-over-one-eye style. 1933 Chicago Mail Order catalog.

Outerwear fashions and the hat styles that go with them. 1933 Chicago Mail Order catalog.

How hat styles are worn with everyday clothing. 1934 Montgomery Ward Specials for Spring and Summer.

Clockwise from upper left: Floral rolled brim Breton Sailor; Lacy braid with organdie flower; Beret and collar set; Sport with bow trim; Sport with artificial leather band; Sport with grosgrain band; Creased crown braid; Peanit straw with two-tone flower. 1934 Montgomery Ward Specials for Spring and Summer.

Clockwise from upper left: Baby Bonnet with organdie flange; Off-the-face straw; Lacy braid with chenille dotted veil; Cuff brim Tricorne; Cotton Gob; Mesh knit cotton with small brim; Rayon knit mesh with novelty ornament; Toyo with scoop brim. 1934 Montgomery Ward Specials for Spring and Summer.

Row (1) Cellophane braid Baby Bonnet; Bagheera visca cloth with flower band; (2) Watteau in pedaline; Crocheted visca Tricorne; Sailor of hand-woven peanit straw; (3) Baby Bonnet in pedaline; Shallow Crown Sailor; Scoop brim of hand-woven peanit straw; Lacy Hemp Tyrolean. 1934 Montgomery Ward catalog.

Clockwise from upper left: Baku weave pedaline straw braid Tricorne; Transparent pyroxylin hair braid; Hemp straw braid Beret; Peanit straw off-the-face; Peanit straw Watteau; Pedaline braid Sailor; Lacy hemp shallow crown Sailor; Hemp straw braid Tyrolean; Stitched brim crepe; Small scoop brim with feather. 1934 Montgomery Ward catalog.

Clockwise from upper left: Tyrolean in pedaline; Panama weave Toyo straw; Pedaline straw braid Turban; Baku weave pedaline straw off-the-face; Shallow crown Sailor; Straw off-the-face; Lacy straw Turban; Pedaline straw braid with feather trim; Baby Bonnet with Tyrolean peaked crown; Sailor with feather trim; Dipped brim in peanit straw. 1934 Montgomery Ward catalog.

Upper left quarter: Rough rayon and cotton crepe Sailor with plaid trim; Visca straw cloth Sailor in checker-board pattern; Crocheted visca straw cloth; Creased crown in peanit straw. Upper right quarter: Waffle weave cotton pique Turban; Draped rayon crepe with mesh veil; Veiled visca cloth; Cuff brim Turban with embroidered veil. Lower right quarter: Forward tipped crown Tyrolean. Lower left quarter: All purpose knock-about of rayon knit; Visca straw cloth Beret. 1934 Montgomery Ward catalog.

Left half, top to bottom: Panama weave Toyo with scarf; Felt wool Crusher; Hand crochet guimpe braid; Creased crown in waffle weave; Rayon and cotton crepe with eyelets and cording. Right half, top to bottom: Cotton pique with stitched brim; Panama weave Toyo straw; Cotton mesh draped Turban; Off-the-face with feather trim; Tyrolean Beret; Rayon and cotton mesh Gob; Peaked Turban; Wool Beret. 1934 Montgomery Ward catalog.

Row (1) Hand-woven peanit straw with a dip over the right eye; Lacy hemp straw braid with tiny mesh veil; Wool felt Crusher; (2) Gob hat of rayon and cotton mesh knit; Snug fitting draped Turban. 1934 Montgomery Ward April 30 sale catalog.

Row (1) Wide brim with front dip; Cotton pique with stitched brim and self bow; Beret of wide wale cotton pique; (2) Shovel brim of wool felt; French Beret; (3) Breton Sailor with turn up stitched brim; Cotton mesh with small brim to shade the eyes; Hand-crocheted Beret of nubby surfaced rayon frill yarn. 1934 Montgomery Ward August 31 sale catalog.

Upper half: Assortment of styles similar to those pictured. No choice of style at clearance price; Lower left: Knitted Softies at clearance price with no choice of style; Lower right: Visca straw cloth Beret; Girls' Beret in lacy hemp straw braid. 1934 Montgomery Ward August 31 sale catalog.

Crochet Your
"Rah-Rah" Hat
Only 39¢

Rah-Rah hat to crochet for yourself. 1934 Montgomery Ward February 28 sale catalog.

Unique plaid patterned sports hat. 1934 Montgomery Ward February 28 sale catalog.

A hairband (hat). 1934 *Needlecraft, The Home Arts Magazine* for November.

Row (1) Wool Beret with suede-like finish; Sailor with a dip over the right eye; (2) Cellophane braid Turban with feather trim; (3) Sailor with stitched brim; Hand-crocheted Beret; Smart new version of a Beret; (4) Snug fitting, hand-draped knit Turban. 1934 Montgomery Ward June 15th sale catalog.

Winning silhouettes for Spring '34. The hat is a tilted bandeau of pedaline straw braid with a silk taffeta bow. 1934 Sears, Roebuck and Co. catalog for Spring and Summer.

Top row: Basque Beret; Shallow molded Beret; (lower left) Plush Zephyr wool Beret for girls & young ladies; (A) Keyring Turban with celluloid ring gathering the top; (B) Crocheted with collapsible crown; (C) Halo to show the forehead; (D) Fitted knit with propeller tucks at the crown. 1934 Sears, Roebuck and Co. catalog for Spring and Summer.

Row (1) Lacy straw Picture; Hand-draped Turban of cellophane millinery cloth; The Deitrich swoops up at the sides and dips down over the eyes; (2) Sailor of nubby bagheera cloth; Halo Turban gives the effect of a thick coil of hair wound around your head; Petal Turban with transparent brim. 1934 Sears, Roebuck and Co. catalog for Spring and Summer.

(A) Dip front wavy brim; (B) Tailored style with telescope crown; (C) Wavy brim in lacy weave; (D) Dipped brim of lacy straw braid; (E) Scoop Sailor of Pedaline braid; (F) Senorita Sailor with marabou pompon; (G) Lift and dip are tailored into this style. Upper right: Veiled Turban with low front dip. 1934 Sears, Roebuck and Co. catalog for Spring and Summer.

(H) Turban with a floral coronet; (J) Lacy weave with floral trim; (K) Off-the-face drooping brim; (L) Go everywhere Turban; (M) Tam Turban of visca cloth; (N) Novelty weave straw braid with lacy edge; (P) Hand-woven straw with large brim. Lower left: Sailor with a garland of gardenias. 1934 Sears, Roebuck and Co. catalog for Spring and Summer.

(A) Up in back, down in front brim with high crown; (B) Forward tilted, military-crowned; (C) Draped Tam with high back and visor brim; (D) Square effect crown and embroidery edged veil; (E) Nautical Overseas cap with tucked crown and modish cuff; (F) Beret with raised back. 1935 Chicago Mail Order catalog.

(A) Overseas cap based on Uncle Sam version; (B) Slanting cuff crown with brim that shortens in the back; (C) High backed, forward slanted veiled Turban. 1935 Chicago Mail Order catalog.

(G) Pinched crown and graceful brim; (H) Velvet Turban with stiffened, veil-like visor; (J) Double up curved brim with chenille dotted veil; (K) Velvet draped roll melts into soft folds at back; (L) Sporty clover topped hat and matching scarf; (M) Dented crown with drooping brim. 1935 Chicago Mail Order catalog.

(G) Winter hat with sloping pointed crown; (H) High-draped and tacked crown with ornaments; (J) Close-fitting Turban with a high, stitched, slantwise cuff; (K) Bell Hop Turban that is high in back and low in front; (L) High backed, visor brimmed velvet Turban; (M) Felt with tucked crown. 1935 Chicago Mail Order catalog.

(G) Tipsy crown that has been tucked; (H) Boat shaped Highland; (J) Toque with ribbon accent and pin; (K) Up in back style with rayon floss tassel; (L) Tucked crown with dip brim; (M) Velvet with scrolls. 1935 Chicago Mail Order catalog.

Latest dress styles and the hats that complement them. 1936 Sears, Roebuck and Co. sale catalog.

In rows, from upper left: (1) Gob softie knit with wheel motif—cotton on one side, pique on the other; (2) Cotton pique with stitched brim and dip over the eye; Beret of hand crochet guimpe braid; Shallow crown Panama. 1935 Montgomery Ward July 31 sale catalog.

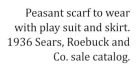

Peasant scarf to wear with play suit and skirt. 1936 Sears, Roebuck and Co. sale catalog.

Matching bandana kerchief to wear with a polka dot beach or play day outfit. 1936 Sears, Roebuck and Co. sale catalog.

Example of popular 1930s Dude Ranch wear. 1938 Pictoral Fashion Book for Summer.

Example of popular 1930s Dude Ranch wear. 1938 Pictoral Fashion Book for Summer.

Don't Be A "One Hat Woman!"

On This Page We Have Photographed the Same Girl Wearing Five Different Hats to Show You How YOU Can Have a New Personality with Each Hat You Select.

HAND WOVEN SISAL STRAW
(A) Be the Spic and Span Summer Girl . . . in this big brim Hat of hand woven imported Sisal, so summery looking and light weight! Let it tilt over your eyes or back on your forehead. Let it dramatize your loveliest costumes. Let it amaze your friends with its high priced look. **$2⁹⁸**

LUSTROUS VISCA CLOTH
(B) Be sophisticated . . . in this hand made Pill Box of Visca and Cellophane cloth; shaded contrasting flowers. Mesh veil. **$1⁹⁸**

CHOICE OF 2 BRAIDS
(C) Be bewitching . . . in this new Poke Bonnet with its short back, creased peak crown and filmy lace veil. **$2⁹⁸**

MILAN-LIKE PEDALINE
(D) Be casual . . . in this wonderfully wearable Swagger Hat. Shiny Pedaline Braid looks like Milan! Two-tone grosgrain; feather. **$1⁴⁹**

NEORA OR PEDALINE
(E) Be debonair . . . in this Hat that sweeps dramatically off your brow. 3-color grosgrain trim. **$2⁹⁸**

HOW TO MEASURE
If hat you select is shown off the face measure your head as in upper photograph, if hat is shown down on forehead measure as in lower photograph. Don't guess your size. Have someone else measure your head. Be sure hat you select is listed in your size.

(A) Straw to tilt over the eyes; (B) Visca cloth Pillbox; (C) Poke Bonnet with short back, creased peak crown and veil; (D) Shiny pedaline braid Swagger; (E) Dramatic sweep. 1938 Montgomery Ward catalog for Spring and Summer.

Row (1) Felt Classic; Off-the-face fur felt; Cuffed Turban; (2) Felt Poke with large drooping brim to shadow the face; Felts side rolled Breton; Off-the-face with creased crown; Breton Sailor with creased crown; (3) Felt Swagger with peaked crown; Perforated felt with high peaked crown; (4) Felt with flat creased crown; Swagger with laced crown. 1938 Montgomery Ward catalog for Spring and Summer.

Clockwise from upper left: Glossy pedaline braid Toque; Bumper brim Turban with veil; Toque with swept forward crown rising to a creased peak; Close-fitting Toque with folded crown; Side sloping Toque with bow and veil; High crown visor Beret. Lower left: (A) Open crown Hindu Turban; (B) Full crown Hindu Turban; (C) Turban with square front; (D) Tucked Halo Turban. 1938 Montgomery Ward catalog for Spring and Summer.

Row (1) Stitched all over droop brim; Off-the-face with three pointed brim; Stitched all over creased crown and droop brim; (2) Stitched all over Breton; High crown sharkskin; Tuscanette braid with droop brim; (3) Panama weave Toyo with changeable band; Swagger Toyo with creased crown and medium brim; Tuscanette braid with turned up back brim. (LR) Tuscanette braid with drooping brim and fruit trim. 1938 Montgomery Ward catalog for Spring and Summer.

(A) Creased forward crown; (B) Straw with contrast flower; (C) Sailor with contrast flowers; (D) Front tilt with turn up brim; (E) Turned up back brim with creased crown; (F) Knitted hat with visor brim; (G) Knitted Gob; (H) Knit with wide stitched brim; (Lower Left) Imported French Beret; (Mid Right) Cotton gabardine Beret; Cotton gabardine Breton Sailor; (Lower Right) Pinwheel sun hat and gloves. 1938 Montgomery Ward catalog for Spring and Summer.

(A) Embroidered veil cascades over the whole hat; (B) Pancho sombrero with chin strap; (C) Shepherdess brim straw with scarf; (D) Flowing brim with soaring crown; (E) Mexican crown Breton. 1939 Chicago Mail Order catalog.

Across top from left: Back veil over crown; Knotted sisal straw with kettle brim; Neora braid with curled brim; (A) Picture in leghorn or sisal straw; (B) Cable edge Pie Plate with flowing scarf to tie or drape around neck; (C) Tip-Tilter with piquant veil; (D) Mushroom Sailor of semi-rough braid. 1939 Chicago Mail Order catalog.

(A) Heart brim with tie; (B) Fluffy finish wool felt with a fuzzy marabou snowball; (C) Bowed Turban; (D) Purl-edge straw with veil; (E) Snood Beret; (F) Shepherdess brim of purl-edge straw; (G) Swagger with Fedora crown. 1939 Chicago Mail Order catalog.

(G) High tipped brim with draping scarf; (H) Pillbox with floral topknot; (J) Tip-tilted Breton with side ribbons; (K) Mushroom Sailor of pedaline braid; (L) Disc Beret with a rayon chenille snood; (M) Wide brim Sailor; (N) Wool felt with a halo of wool embroidery; (P) Bumper with veiling bow; (Q) High-crowned hat borrowed from the gaucho; (R) Self-laced Sombrero; (S) Flower laden hat of medium rough braid. 1939 Chicago Mail Order catalog.

(H) Forward swooping Breton with cascading wimple; (J) Fancy braid with bonnet brim; (K) High Tiara Turban of hand-draped rayon crepe; (L) Salad Bowl Breton of semi-rough straw; (M) Off-the-face style with exotic flowers; (N) Bumper edge Sailor for sporty wear; (P) Forward sweep of fine pedaline braid; (R) Off-the-face style with 4-color rayon jersey streamers; (S) Swagger with up or down brim; (T) Tip-tilted Watteau with 2-color veiling; (U) Picture with wide, drooping brim. 1939 Chicago Mail Order catalog.

Lines With a Lift

IN THE UP-SWEPT BRIM OF YOUR BRETON SAILOR

(B) There's a saucy tilt and a "Bandbox" luster to this glossy Breton of Sharkskin—the handsome (synthetic) straw body. Perky 2-tone bows. New head-hugging mesh snood. **$1 39**

(A) Colors: Navy, Gray 806, Paris Tan 925 or White. **$1 00 EA.**

Perfect in Pedaline Grand in Felt

(C) Wear a new Breton with a pert, pointed crown. Tip it forward roguishly and draw the shirred elastic ribbon over your hair. Three flowers on top; a clever bow at the side. Fine Pedaline braid resembling Milan straw. **$1 59**

(D) Rough straws are newest! And this glossy, rough-weave Breton can't be excelled for tailored smartness. "Upped" brim and stiffened rayon taffeta bow. Wide taffeta band fits over the hair. Reproduction of a $5.00 style. **$1 49**

Choice of Pedaline or Felt

CLASSIC FELT $1 59

Our finest felt! A grand easy-to-wear style that gives modern up-to-dateness to young heads and old. Brim is just wide enough for flattery. Style and quality are the kind usually found only in big city shops at very high prices. You save money at Sears, always.

(E) Genuine knotted Sisol straw! Usually in $5.00 hats. Has a sheer, finely nubbed texture. Beautiful quality, hand woven. Flattering brim; soft ribbons. **$1 79**

(F) The brim turns back dramatically as if to say "See this pretty face!" Sparkling Pedaline braid with dainty flowers and a deep, lovely veil. **$1 39**

(G) The flattery of an eye shading brim in a small, trim hat! Soft veil and tinted flowers. **$1 79 EA.**

(A) Breton Sailor with upswept brim; (B) Sharkskin Breton with mesh snood; (C) Breton with pointed crown; (D) Rough weave Breton with upped brim; (E) Knotted sisal straw with large brim; (F) Dramatic turn back brim; (G) Eye shading brim; Lower left: Classic felt. 1939 Sears, Roebuck and Co. catalog for Spring and Summer.

Row (1) Sloping crown and drooping brim; Woven rustic straw Pillbox; Rough straw with shirred Rayon jersey facing in dark contrast; Rough straw wide hat with matching bag; (2) Patent Milan straw with bonnet shaped crown and flower-trimmed brim; Rough straw braid with distinctive tall crown; Milan straw with colorful berries; Leghorn Bonnet with Sweetheart brim. 1939 Sears, Roebuck and Co. catalog for Spring and Summer.

Row 1: (A) Thong laced brim edge can be rolled any way you like; (B) Tyrolean felt; (C) Felt Pork Pie with snap brim; Row 2: Rough straw Sailor; Knotted sisal with pencil rolled edge; Tiny hat that tilts forward; Sisal straw Bonnet with ribbon ties. 1939 Sears, Roebuck and Co. catalog for Spring and Summer.

Upper left: (A) Neora braid with floral bandeau; (B) Pedaline braid with brim that turns up in front and back; Wide brim of flexible straw. Clockwise from center left: Pedaline braid with the basket weave cellophane banded crown; Dainty Pie Plate with tiny peak on top; Pie Plate with deep crown; Rayon faille ribbon Tam; Sewn rayon grosgrain ribbon; Spring weight felt with peek-a-boo brim; French Beret; Tiny, round, and flat to tip forward. 1939 Sears, Roebuck and Co. catalog for Spring and Summer.

(A) Tilt it recklessly – the snood holds it on; (B) Tiny crown with two tone bow; (C) Two way brim; Clockwise from center left: Classic style of pedaline braid; Pedaline braid with watteau brim; Lilting brim with shaped crown; Sailor with tilted brim tailored so the crown continues below the brim in the back; Felt with a tall crown and dipped brim; Tuscan-like braid with large brim; Off-the-face tucked rayon crepe. 1939 Sears, Roebuck and Co. catalog for Spring and Summer.

CHAPTER 4: 1940 TO 1949

Bonnets Star in "GONE WITH the WIND"

The bonnet's back—prettiest fashion of the 19th century gets a royal welcome along with Clark Gable, Vivien Leigh and Olivia de Havilland in "Gone with the Wind," Metro-Goldwyn-Mayer's David O. Selznick production.

Ⓐ The Beau-Catcher Bonnet
$1 98 "Gone With the Wind" demonstrates the charm of the style. Glossy, beautiful rough straw. Double bow of rich rayon moire ribbon.

Ⓑ Scarlett O'Hara Bonnet
$1 98 Vivien Leigh looks lovely in a style like this; so will you! Brim turns up or down; forehead band may be worn high or low. Fine rough straw braid. Rayon velvet ribbons.

Two Hats in One!
$1 00 A charming bonnet! But slip back the brim and it's off-the-face. All wool spring weight felt; laced edge. Fine rayon and cotton grosgrain.

The Poke Bonnet
$1 00 Frames your face in a wide high sweep; the effect is bewitching! Tuscan-like braid: rayon and cotton grosgrain trim.

The "Heartbreaker"
$1 59 The kind of hat men like...feminine, pretty, gay! Dips low at front; rayon veil ties under chin, if you like. Fine rough straw braid.

Choice—Braid, Felt
$1 19 Colors: Blue Violet 820, Coral 456, Navy Blue, Tango Rust 408, White.

Smart up or down Brim

The Perfect Casual Hat
$1 69 Soft Wool Felt or Rough Straw Braid

A good looking hat—with soft, wide brim and an easy-to-wear crown that's definitely correct style. Smart shops ask very high prices for hats of this grade. Buy at the sensible Kerrybrooke price, put them side by side, and it's hard to tell the difference! Summer weight wool felt, or rough straw braid. Smart many-way brim.

(A) Based on a style from the movie *Gone With the Wind*; (B) Based on a style from the movie "Gone With the Wind" with up or down brim. Row (2) Brim worn down or back off-the-face; Poke with high sweep brim in front; Straw braid with dipping brim; Braid or felt with up or down brim; (3) Braid or felt casual. 1940 Sears, Roebuck and Co. catalog for Spring and Summer.

Row (1) Wasp waist crown with bustle back; Straw or felt with small crown; (2) Side roll with tassel; Suit Hat; Veiled Homburg in glossy braid; Pedaline braid with extra wide band and streamers; (3) Pedaline braid with visor and ribbon back bow; Straw braid with small crown; Rough straw braid with brim that curves up at the sides; Pedaline braid with small crown and full veil. 1940 Sears, Roebuck and Co. catalog for Spring and Summer.

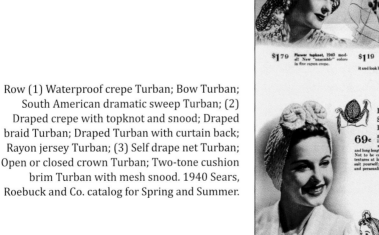

Row (1) Waterproof crepe Turban; Bow Turban; South American dramatic sweep Turban; (2) Draped crepe with topknot and snood; Draped braid Turban; Draped Turban with curtain back; Rayon jersey Turban; (3) Self drape net Turban; Open or closed crown Turban; Two-tone cushion brim Turban with mesh snood. 1940 Sears, Roebuck and Co. catalog for Spring and Summer.

New Young Bretons

Uptilted brims... lines with a lilt
Designed to be pretty... side, front and back

Shiny Rough Straw With Snood
$1⁴⁹ Ⓐ New as tomorrow's news! Rayon mesh snood back, shallow crown, young, wide brim... so many important fashion points! Comes in lovely rough straw braid with that glossy richness that keeps its new look through long wear! Ideal with suits, print dresses. Rayon and cotton grosgrain trim.

New... the 1940 Profile Breton
$1⁴⁹ Ⓑ Youth in every line! Fashion in every detail! Notice the high lifted line at the side; it's remarkable what it does for your profile. Fluted brim, up-shooting feather; patent milan straw. Deep crown fits down well.

$1⁶⁹ Actual $2.98 value! Stunning nubbed sisal straw, new, fine-textured. Pencil-rolled brim —another expensive, unusual detail.

$1⁵⁹ New "Watteau" breton! Gay, dressy! Deeply fitted back. Pedaline braid; rayon and cotton grosgrain trim; rayon velvet flower.

$1⁰⁰ Any-age, any-day hat. Popular because it's so becoming! Pedaline braid; rayon and cotton grosgrain trim. Blending flowers.

$1⁰⁰ Felt or Pedaline Braid. So popular we offer choice Each of fine Wool Felt or Imported Pedaline Braid. Cotton mesh snood.

Cushion Brims, Height-Giving Trimming... Four Exciting New Fashions

$1⁶⁹ Plaid bustle back! Grand for suits or dress-up! Flattering rolled edge brim in place of a brim. Pedaline braid; rayon plaid ribbon bustle bow. Rayon veil. It's smart, becoming!

$1⁶⁹ Bows and blossoms! Forward .. tilt! Straw-like cellophane braid in a smart pillbox that looks twice the price! Softening, flattering cushion brim; rayon veil ties in a gay, height-giving bow. So easy to wear!

$1⁶⁹ Gay back interest in a postilion that takes advantage of the becomingness of a cushion brim. Fine quality, beautifully made flowers and rayon veil. Pedaline braid styled with 1940's "forward" crown.

$1¹⁹ A hi-fashion! A joy to own and wear! Rayon and cotton grosgrain; rough straw braid.

Row (1) Rough straw Breton with snood; Profile Breton with high lifted line at side; (2) Nubbed straw Breton with pencil rolled brim; Watteau Breton; Straw Breton with floral trim; Felt or pedaline braid Breton with snood; (3) Plaid bustle back with rolled edge brim; Cellophane braid Pillbox; Forward veiled crown with cushion brim; Rough straw braid with grosgrain ribbon trim. 1940 Sears, Roebuck and Co. catalog for Spring and Summer.

Row (1) Straw braid with cuff brim and puff bow; Cushion brim molded in rough straw braid; Rough straw braid with ribbon streamers; (2) Pedaline braid with ribbon and flower trim; Braid Breton with feather trim; Braid with trimmings; (3) Flexible pedaline braid or felt; Braid with cushion brim; Tricorne with lifted brim; Braid with medium brim and bustle bow. 1940 Sears, Roebuck and Co. catalog for Spring and Summer.

Young Looking Hats

"Beautiful Lady" Hat
$1⁹⁸ In a class with $5.00 and $7.50 hats! Elegance in every detail... in its fine imported Swiss Straw braid, in its style and workmanship, in its skillful design! Cuff brim has the high lifted line that does so much to give you a slim, young look. Puff bow of rayon veiling adds height and distinction. Rayon velvet leaves come in colors that flatter your complexion. The whole hat has a queenly air about it... your friends will admire you in it. Wear it for parties and important occasions.

$1³⁹ "Success-fashion." Cushion-trimmed hat molded in smart rough straw braid. Rayon veiling; summer flowers. Fits comfortably.

$1⁵⁹ Youth and fashion come first in Sears hats; here's proof! Rough straw braid, popular style. Rayon and cotton grosgrain streamers. Rayon and Cotton Flowers.

88ᶜ Buy it early, wear it late. Pedaline braid; complimentary brim. Rayon and cotton grosgrain ribbon and flowers.

$1⁴⁹ Feather trimmed! One of the most becoming bretons you've ever worn! Fine Pedaline braid, pencil-curled brim.

$1⁸⁹ Dignified, becoming to mature women, and yet it's so smart! Fine Pedaline braid, richly trimmed.

$1¹⁹ Colors: Black, Navy, Red Each Wine 514, White.

$1⁷⁹ Good style — and most becoming! Especially nice Pedaline braid. Youthful cushion brim; softening in effect; easy to wear. Tailored quill; rayon veil, generously used.

$1⁷⁹ 1940's best tricorne. The secret of its charm is in its clever width, the lifted brim, the graceful height. It's so becoming. Rayon velvet leaves make a rich trimming on soft flexible Pedaline braid. Fine Rayon veiling tied in a puffy bow at the back.

$1⁸⁹ New interest in its deep fitted back, its bustle bow of rayon and cotton grosgrain and, for a finishing touch, its ribbon edged rayon veiling. Fine Pedaline braid; flattering medium brimline. It's charming.

Row (1) Felt bowed Beret with chenille dot veiling and elastic snood; Winged bird topped Pillbox with snood; Shirred velvet Boater with elastic snood; Feather bird accent on Toque with elastic snood; (2) Homburg creased crown Postilion; Flat crown Postilion with side rolled brim; Pointed crown Postilion; High crown Postilion with shirred detailing and swirling brim. 1939-40 Montgomery Ward catalog for Fall and Winter.

Upper left: Felt with muffin brim and feather; Felt with tiny platform crown; Bottom row: Tiny crown Cloche with elastic snood; Felt with pencil curl brim, tiny crown and band snood; Tiny crown Bumper with elastic snood; Turret crown, pencil curl brim, veil and snood. 1939-40 Montgomery Ward catalog for Fall and Winter.

Row (1) Peaked crown velvet with matching muff; Velvet tucked bumper brim; Velvet tucked Turban; (2) Felt Toque with generous mesh veil; Felt Bumper with snood; Felt Shako with bow and snood; (3) Felt Pillbox with wimple; Felt Tricorne with generous veil; Toque with self bow and veil; Felt Toque with embroidered veil. 1939-40 Montgomery Ward catalog for Fall and Winter.

Row (1) Roll brim Swagger with Tyrolean crown; Veiled felt; Felt Swagger; (2) Beret with ostrich feather; Felt Tricorne with tucked brim; Felt Toque with velvet band; (3) Classic felt with tucked crown; Felt with lifted back brim and veil; Classic with flat creased crown; Felt with side roll brim and creased crown. 1939-40 Montgomery Ward catalog for Fall and Winter.

The perfect "coat-suit" hats

Soft-Shirred Brim. Note the expensive, hand-detail on the brim of this dashing classic Hat. Made of good quality soft, supple Fur Felt, cleverly manipulated telescoped crown and the becoming down-swept brim. Grosgrain ribbon band, bow in back.

Winged Pill Box for the new "hair-do's". New Wool felt with two feather wings, mesh veil.

The Padre Sailor. Supple Fur Felt with curved brim, low crown, contrasting feathers and a mesh veil for trimming.

Tailored Type Bonnet combines classic lines with face-framing flattery. Big brim laced all around, swept up in back to leave room for your collar. Of good quality Felt (94% New Wool, 6% Casein fiber). Banded in grosgrain with a bow in back.

Profile Hat of good quality New Wool Felt. Grosgrain ribbon, colorful feather trim.

The New Sailor, right with any costume. Good quality New Wool Felt, its low crown trimmed with smart feathers, grosgrain ribbon and mesh veiling.

Row (1) Fur felt classic style with shirred brim; Felt Pillbox with feather wings on either side; Padre Sailor with curved brim and low crown; (2) Tailored Bonnet with laced brim; Felt Profile with feather trim; Felt Sailor with low crown. 1941-42 Montgomery Ward catalog for Fall and Winter.

Pompadour or Bangs look well with this kettle edge brim Bonnet. New Wool Felt, matching grosgrain ribbon trim.

Attractive Bonnet with rounded crown, curved brim. New Wool Felt, matching grosgrain band and bow.

Copy of a Costly Hat. Off-the-face Bonnet of New Wool Felt with contrasting grosgrain band and motif.

Sweetheart Bonnet with graceful dipped brim. New Wool Felt, contrasting ribbon trim, mesh veil.

Mexico Inspired This Bonnet. New Wool Felt with novel creased crown, and matching grosgrain band and flange around the brim.

New Wool Felt in a classic cloche-bonnet that's a "Natural" for casual and sports clothes. Grand value.

Lifted Squared Brim rising above a smooth band, adds a young look to this New Wool Felt bonnet. Grosgrain band, bow, binding.

The Big Shirred Brim sweeps up to frame the face dramatically in one of the smartest All New Wool Felt Cloth Hats. Self bow in back.

The Brim Turns Up to give this hat its smart new look. New Wool Felt with novel creased crown, grosgrain band with bow in front. Mesh veil.

How to Measure. After you select the hat you want, notice the angle at which it is worn in the illustration. Then measure your head at that angle, as shown in the sketch as above. Number of inches is your head-size. Do not make allowances.

Drama is the Keynote of the fashion season, and it's the feature of this beautiful Par-Felt hat. Off-the-face style, its brim up-swept in a graceful flare, its creased crown is deep in back to fit comfortably with coat collar or suit. Perfect to show off your new hair-do be it bangs or pompadour. Right with your dressiest daytime clothes. Grosgrain flange and contrasting trim.

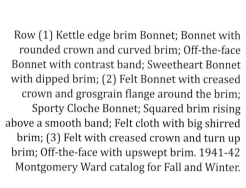

Row (1) Kettle edge brim Bonnet; Bonnet with rounded crown and curved brim; Off-the-face Bonnet with contrast band; Sweetheart Bonnet with dipped brim; (2) Felt Bonnet with creased crown and grosgrain flange around the brim; Sporty Cloche Bonnet; Squared brim rising above a smooth band; Felt cloth with big shirred brim; (3) Felt with creased crown and turn up brim; Off-the-face with upswept brim. 1941-42 Montgomery Ward catalog for Fall and Winter.

Row (1) Beaver finish felt with novel crown; Beaver finish felt Bonnet; (2) Felt Cloche; Padre Sailor with grosgrain band and feathers; Felt with flowers and feather trim; Fur felt Cloche with floral trim; (3) Felt Profile with feather pierced crown; Veiled felt Cloche with a feather poised in the crown; Padre Sailor with metal ornaments in front; Felt Homburg with telescope crown. 1941-42 Montgomery Ward catalog for Fall and Winter.

Row (1) Tucked Pillbox with deep back; Pie Plate style with back headband; (2) Pillbox to wear with your pompadour hairstyle; Felt Turban with feather wings and band; Velvet fan front Turban; Topknot Turban; (3) Felt Toque with floral wreath; Off-the-face Toque; Draped velvet Turban; Tucked velvet Turban. 1941-42 Montgomery Ward catalog for Fall and Winter.

Row (1) Big brim Classic; Felt with telescoped flat crown with pierced ornament; Curved brim Sailor; (2) Classic felt with snap brim; Felt with creased crown and large brim; Felt with creased crown and grosgrain cascade of bows; Classic with creased stitched crown and scoop brim; (3) Off-the-face Classic with scoop brim; Pork Pie with creased telescope crown; Felt snap brim; Bonnet with creased crown and scoop brim. 1941-42 Montgomery Ward catalog for Fall and Winter.

(A) Felt with hackle feathers to cap the ears; (B) Sloped crown Pillbox with wing feathers; (D) Head hugging with three self feather flowers capping each ear; (E) Dressmaker felt with tiny bunches of felt bananas on either side; (F) Side pleat half-hat; (G) Head hugging Matador braided over the ears; (H) Molded felt with pleated top; (J) Calot crown with triple ruffle front; (K) Felt Coolie Beret with golden nail heads; (L) Ruffled Pompadour half-hat with full veil; (M) Bejeweled velvet Calot; (N) Crocheted Pompadour Pillbox; (P) Anti-macasser shaped to fit the head with twin pompons; (R) Half-hat with self rosettes; (S) Felt Dutch Cap. 1944-45 Sears, Roebuck and Co. catalog for Fall and Winter.

(A) Wool felt with turned down casablanca brim and little crown; (B) Wool felt with muffin brim; (C) Bonnet with sharply dipped brim and creased crown; (D) Wool or fur felt with double stitching around brim; (E) Wool felt with laced crown and embossed brim; (F) Wool felt with large stitched Breton brim; (G) Side drape Cloche; (H) Telescope crown and wide front brim with gathered stitching; (J) Topper Cloche with short back to clear a coat collar; (K) Tricorne Pompadour with cuffed brim; (L) Wool felt wide brim casual; (M) Wool felt with Sweetheart brim and wispy veil. 1944-45 Sears, Roebuck and Co. catalog for Fall and Winter.

(A) Wool felt with Beret brim and veil; (B) Awning brim Sailor with velvet petals; (C) Watteau brim that rises at back; (D) Puffed-edge little hat to wear forward or back of your pompadour; (E) Wool felt with reinforced kettle-edge and lifted sides; (F) Watteau Profile with manipulated brim; (G) Draped Profile Turban with side swirl; (H) Tam Turban with feather quills; (J) Draped Turban with rolled top; (K) Small brim, upturned in back, with a wispy veil; (L) Double brim Visor of wool felt; (M) Tailored brim with upturned back. 1944-45 Sears, Roebuck and Co. catalog for Fall and Winter.

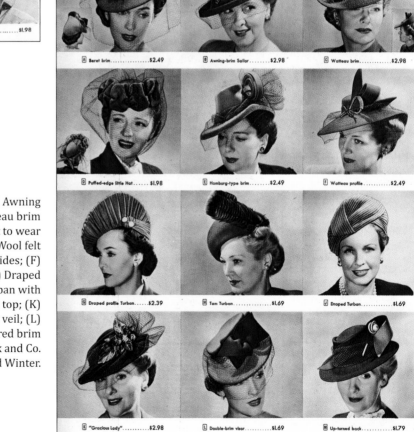

(A) Felt with dip brim; (B) Felt with creased crown and brim turned up in back; (C) Bandeau mounted brim that turns up in back; (D) Felt narrow brim; (E) Tilted bandeau with dipped brim; (F) Aureole Beret is hand-draped in back; (G) Rolled brim for up or down with pompon and feather through the creased crown; (H) Off-the-face with slashed brim; (J) Felt with 3-way tuck in the crown. 1944-45 Sears, Roebuck and Co. catalog for Fall and Winter.

(1) Daisies; (2) Feather gardenia; (3) Gardenia; (4) Bow; (5) Sequin butterfly; (6) Feather morning glories; (7) Roses; (8) Feather carnations; (9) Bow; (10) Feather pompon; (11) Gardenia and bow; (12) Violets; (13) and (14) Lilly Dache nets (snoods). Nets can be worn alone, or with ornaments shown; (15) Gardenia cluster; (16) Gardenia cluster; (17) Rosebuds; (18) Glamour combs. 1945 Montgomery Ward catalog for Spring and Summer.

Clockwise from upper left: Knit French Beret; Knitted, waterproof Beret with elastic band; Made to order Beret; Chieftiel Beret with quill; Initial Beret with forward drape; Knitted Scotty Tam; Angora Beret; Felt Hat with turned up brim; Cotton double texture stocking cap; Felt Casual; Knitted Casual; Draped Beret with pompon and ascot scarf; Crocheted Beret; Knitted wool Beret with visor; Knitted wool Beret. 1944-45 Sears, Roebuck and Co. catalog for Fall and Winter.

(14) Square scarf; (15) Rayon mesh Turban; (16) Halo Half-Turban; (17) Crocheted Cotton Half hat; (18) Cotton mesh Dutch cap; (19) Rayon jersey Halo; (20) Hand-crocheted Calot; Lower left inset: (14) Draped Toque with deep back; (15) Forward Toque with wired bow and soft flowers; (16) Winged Toque with feather band and feather wings; (17) Straw braid with flower trim; (18) Felt Bumper; (19) Dimpled Beret. 1945 Montgomery Ward catalog for Spring and Summer.

(1) Faille Calot with heart shaped ruffle; (2) Rayon crepe hand-draped Turban; (3) Synthetic straw braid Profile; (4) Cloche with shirred net ruching around the creased crown; (5) Tucked Beret with matching bag; (6) Flower topped Bumper; (7) Felt Classic; (8) Rayon jersey intricately draped Turban; (9) Synthetic straw braid Toque; (10) Synthetic straw braid Classic; (11) Shiny synthetic straw braid Toque. 1945 Montgomery Ward catalog for Spring and Summer.

(13) Calot with flower clusters; (14) Rosette Calot with snood effect; (15) Cushion brim Bonnet; (16) Bumper Beret; (17) Felt Bumper; (18) Felt Calot with felt florals; (19) Basket weave synthetic straw braid Calot; (20) Rosette Beret with feathers; (21) Dutch hat that opens flat; (22) Hand-crocheted Pillbox; (23) Hand-crocheted Calot of celtagel fiber; (24) Muffin Beret. 1945 Montgomery Ward catalog for Spring and Summer.

(C) Off-the-face Beret with ostrich feather pompon; (D) Felt Tricorne Bumper with ribbon bustle; (E) Felt Off-the-face with blouse crown and taffeta bows; (F) Wool yarn needlepoint classic Cloche with self fringe. 1947-48 Montgomery Ward catalog for Fall and Winter.

Becoming Is The Word

(1) Braided Halo Brim and back bow of grosgrain ribbon, flattering on a crown of shiny Visca Straw Cloth.

(2) Summery Sailor. Smartly shaped of imported basket weave Straw Braid, with a becoming downturned brim, and wide grosgrain ribbon band, bow motif.

(3) Young and Pretty . . . this charming Toque of dainty, rich looking flowers has a stiffened ribbon bow, mesh veil and grosgrain headband for fit.

(4) Mushroom Brim Bonnet with flattering flare, and deep back crown for comfortable fit. Made of better quality New Wool Felt.

(5) Ever-Popular Calot in a flattering new version, decoratively trimmed with four large self flowers. Of good New Wool Felt. Has self covered pin.

(6) Forward Bumper . . . Of better quality New Wool Felt. Especially charming with felt flowers stitched at each side, felt band, dainty mesh veil.

1.98   2.98

(7) Chetnik Beret. Attractive in soft, pliable novel weave synthetic Straw Braid. Has two pretty self rosettes on the side. Wear it at a becoming angle.

(8) Classic Tucked Beret . . . Fashion's choice for tailored clothes. Of good sturdy Rayon and Cotton Faille, with grosgrain ribbon bow at back. Very smart and trim and most becoming.

2.98   1.69

(9) Off-The-Face Bonnet with gracefully curved brim, flower trim. Of imported basket weave Straw Braid.

(10) Pill Box of transparent synthetic Hair Braid sewed row-on-row with synthetic Straw Braid. 4 self rosettes.

(1) Braided Halo brim; (2) Basket weave straw braid Sailor; (3) Floral laden Toque; (4) Mushroom brim Bonnet; (5) Calot with self flowers; (6) Felt Forward Bumper; (7) Chetnik Beret with self rosettes at side; (8) Tucked Beret; (9) Off-the-face Bonnet; (10) Transparent synthetic hair braid Pillbox. 1945 Montgomery Ward catalog for Spring and Summer.

(A) Felt Toque with ostrich plumes; (B) Felt Profile Beret with novel glitters; (C) Felt Beret with satin bows; (D) Felt rolled brim Breton; (E) Crocheted felt cloth Profile Toque; (F) Felt Cloche with satin bows and feathers; (G) Telescope crown Breton with ribbon trim and veil; (H) Sequined felt Calot with veil; (J) Deep back bumper Beret; (K) Creased crown Homburg with satin band and bows. 1947-48 Montgomery Ward catalog for Fall and Winter.

(L) Felt peaked brim Bonnet with glittered feathers; (M) Draped felt Cloche; (N) Sequin mesh over velvet Calot; (P) Velvet Sailor with self ruffle; (R) Velvet draped Turban with glitter trim; (T) Felt creased brim Bumper; (U) Felt Derby with mesh overlay crown; (V) Felt rolled brim Padre with sequin trim; (W) Felt Toque with feather trim; (X) Felt creased crown Toque with bow and streamers. 1947-48 Montgomery Ward catalog for Fall and Winter.

(L) Felt high crown Homburg with quills; (M) Felt ripple brim Bonnet with velvet bows and feathers; (N) Creased crown Breton with ribbon band and back streamers; (P) Creased crown Bumper with sequin design; (R) Off-the-face Pillbox with sequin band; (T) Felt Scottie Bumper with feather trim; (U) Cloche with satin loops and glittering nail heads; (V) Metallic braid Calot with circular veil; (W) Felt Casual with veil; (X) Creased crown Cloche with tri-color braided band. 1947-48 Montgomery Ward catalog for Fall and Winter.

(M) Deep crown Cloche with feather cluster; (N) Felt Tricorne with ostrich feather; (P) High crown Cloche with feather trim; (R) Felt Bonnet with satin bows; (T) Deep back Beret with back floral and bow trim; (U) Felt Homburg with mesh veil; (V) Felt Padre with ribbon rosettes; (W) Creased crown Cloche with metallic and felt braided band; (X) Visor brim Toque with feather trim; (Y) High creased crown Cloche; (Z) Laced crown Casual with novel stitching on brim and crown. 1947-48 Montgomery Ward catalog for Fall and Winter.

(A) Off-the-face side swept silhouette; (B) Felt Plateau with veiling around the crown; (C) Off-the-face with a bloused crown; (D) Draped Turban with pleated cuff; (E) Forward tilted Coachman with ostrich pompon; (F) Profile with 1-sided feather detail; (G) Draped Sailor with dressmaker cuff; (H) Platform Scottie with high crown and ostrich plume; (J) Felt side drape dips on one side. 1948 Sears, Roebuck and Co. catalog for Fall and Winter.

(A) Beret with pheasant feather and quills; (B) Draped Buccaneer brim that is wide at sides and has a pleated front; Row (2) Off-the-face ripple silhouette with satin loops; Bow back fur cuff; Felt with Halo brim; Glistening feathers massed in a putt; Row (3) Oversized back bow on an Off-the-face felt; Felt Scotty with feathers; Side dip felt with satin flower; Sailor with maline pouf at front. 1948 Sears, Roebuck and Co. catalog for Fall and Winter.

(A) Felt Tricorne with satin back drapes; (B) Rounded brim felt with ostrich plume; (C) Quilled felt Casual; Row (2) Plateau Sailor with double-tiered brim; Velvet Turban; Plumed Postilion with pencil roll edge; Bustle bow Bonnet with Off-the-face brim; (3) Bow-knot Bumper with sequin band; Felt Bonnet with pleated frill of chenille dotted maline around crown; Scalloped cuff Half hat with satin loops; Dutch Bonnet with flaring brim. 1948 Sears, Roebuck and Co. catalog for Fall and Winter.

(A) Swirling feathers around a velvet crown; (B) Felt with full crown and butterfly bow; Row (2) Sailor with bloused crown and quill wing; Plumed Postilion with rising crown and rolled brim; Scottie with sequin band and satin back bow; Felt with up curved brim and deep crown; (3) Felt Coachman Derby with satin band and bow; Watteau with ostrich pompon; Bumper with feather top-knot; Shako Pillbox with veil. 1948 Sears, Roebuck and Co. catalog for Fall and Winter.

Hat example shown with current suit to sew at home. 1948 Advance Pattern #4655.

$1.84 TIERED TURBAN; new off-the-face style at a tempting Kerrybrooke price. Wool felt; self bow in back: dressy ornaments in front.	**$1.09** BLOUSED CROWN VISOR CAP; the flattering fashion that's all the rage with smart girls everywhere . . . at a money-saving Sears price. 70% wool, 30% cotton felt; self stick-up on crown.	**$2.33** DASHING SAILOR; newest Kerrybrooke headliner; wins raves from the young crowd. Wool felt; grosgrain band; smart double quills. Rayon veil.	**$2.34** DEMURE BONNET, a compliment-winning wool felt charmer with lots of fashion news in its flattering, irregular brim; rayon taffeta loops.
$1.79 PINWHEEL CALOT, such a gay little gadabout . . . nice on any hairdo, with any outfit. A Kerrybrooke value in embossed wool felt; self bows; hat pin.	**$2.29** DIP-BRIM CASUAL; has-grosgrain band with metal spangles for a dressed-up look. Wool felt.	**$2.19** SCOTTIE HALF-HAT; becoming and easy-to-wear with its tiered crown, cocky feather quills. Wool felt with self-covered wire headsize loop.	**$1.98** SAUCY DERBY, pretty and feminine with its soft rolled edge, flyaway grosgrain streamers. A typical Kerrybrooke value. Wool felt.
$1.98 IMPORTED BASQUE BERET, always flattering; good any season, with any outfit. Kerrybrooke 100% wool; well made for good fit, easy draping.	**$1.84** SLICK LITTLE HELMET; head-hugging hat . . perfect with the new softer, long-skirted fashions. Wool felt with pleated crown	**$1.74** POPULAR BRETON; fun-to-wear style that pairs happily with suits, coats. Wool felt; hat pin .	**$1.49** BOW-AND-FLOWER CALOT, one of your favorite Kerrybrookes with a new look; a low price. Wool felt; four self bows and flowers; gold color metal nailheads.

Row (1) Off-the-face tiered Turban; Bloused crown visor Cap; Felt Sailor with quills and veil; Felt Bonnet with irregular brim; (2) Pinwheel Calot with self bows; Dip brim felt Casual; Scottie Half-hat with quills; Derby with flyaway streamers; (3) Basque Beret; Felt Helmet with pleated crown; Felt Breton; Felt Calot with self bows and flowers. 1948 Sears, Roebuck and Co. catalog for Fall and Winter.

Popular style of crochet hat and bag set. 1949 "Ideas for Gifts" from the Spool Cotton Co.

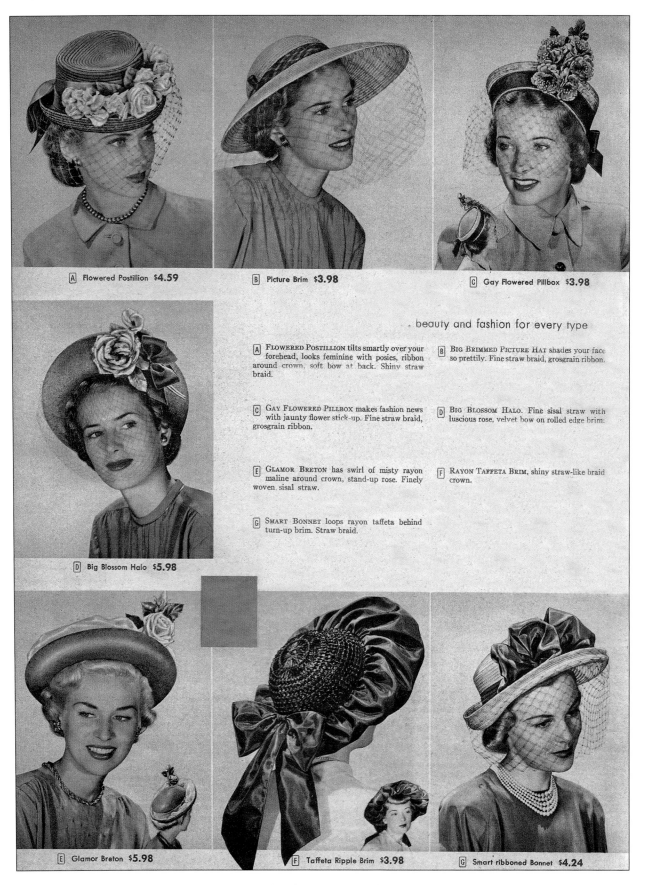

A | Flowered Postillion $4.59

B | Picture Brim $3.98

C | Gay Flowered Pillbox $3.98

beauty and fashion for every type

A | FLOWERED POSTILLION tilts smartly over your forehead, looks feminine with posies, ribbon around crown, soft bow at back. Shiny straw braid.

B | BIG BRIMMED PICTURE HAT shades your face so prettily. Fine straw braid, grosgrain ribbon.

C | GAY FLOWERED PILLBOX makes fashion news with jaunty flower stick-up. Fine straw braid, grosgrain ribbon.

D | BIG BLOSSOM HALO. Fine sisal straw with luscious rose, velvet bow on rolled edge brim.

E | GLAMOR BRETON has swirl of misty rayon maline around crown, stand-up rose. Finely woven sisal straw.

F | RAYON TAFFETA BRIM, shiny straw-like braid crown.

G | SMART BONNET loops rayon taffeta behind turn-up brim. Straw braid.

D | Big Blossom Halo $5.98

E | Glamor Breton $5.98

F | Taffeta Ripple Brim $3.98

G | Smart ribboned Bonnet $4.24

(A) Forehead tilt Postillion with flowers; (B) Straw braid Picture with veil; (C) Pillbox with flower stick-up; (D) Sisal straw with rose on rolled edge brim; (E) Breton with rayon swirl around crown and stand up rose; (F) Shirred taffeta brim on a straw braid crown; (G) Turn up brim Bonnet with taffeta loops. 1949 Sears, Roebuck and Co. catalog for Spring and Summer.

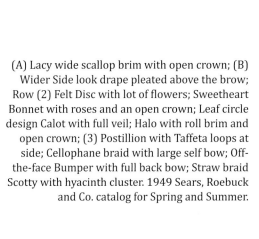

DRAMATIC SHAPES, exquisitely trimmed . . . unusual at these prices

[A] PLATEAU BONNET, lavishly veiled with dotted chenille. Feather-light sisal straw.

[B] WIDE BRIM has sheer flattery of row-on-row edging, mesh veiling over open crown. Sisal straw.

[C] EXQUISITE FLOWER HALO. Sheer maline covers blossoms. Open crown. Strawlike cloth.

[D] COCKADE OF VEILING is saucy stick-up on brim of tiny breton. Fine straw braid.

[E] BRIGHT STRIPES, SIDE BOW. Profile brim with wonderful Roman-striped rayon ribbon. Fine sisal straw.

[F] SWEETHEART RUFFLE. Dotted rayon maline, open crown. Straw-like cloth.

HOW-TO-MEASURE . . draw tape measure around part of head you wear hat. Number of inches is correct size.

[G] HUGE WHITE ROSES, high at side of flattering off-the-face profile brim. Edges are wired and bound with the same grosgrain ribbon that bands crown. Featherlight sisal straw.

[A] Plateau Bonnet $5.98   [B] Wide Sweep Brim $5.98   [C] Flower Halo $5.94   [D] Cockade Breton $3.98   [E] Bright Stripes . . Side Bow $5.98   [F] Frilly Sweetheart Ruffle $3.49   [G] High Roses, Profile-Brim $5.98

(A) Plateau Bonnet with dotted chenille veil; (B) Wide brim with mesh veiling over an open crown; (C) Flower laden Halo with open crown; (D) Cockade of veiling adorns a Breton; (E) Profile with band of striped rayon ribbon that ties to the side; (F) Dotted maline sweetheart ruffle adorns an open crown; (G) Profile brim with huge roses high at the side. 1949 Sears, Roebuck and Co. catalog for Spring and Summer.

IT'S THE PRETTY HAT
that does the most for you

[A] LACY, WIDE SCALLOPED BRIM. Starched straw-like braid, rayon taffeta ribbon.

[B] LOVELY WIDE-SIDE LOOK. Shiny straw braid drape-pleated smartly above your brow. Grosgrain ribbon band, loops and streamers.

$4.39 $4.29

$2.74 — LUSCIOUS FLOWERS top felt disc. (70% wool, 30% cotton). Rayon taffeta trim. Back loop for comfortable fit.

$3.74 — SWEETHEART BONNET. Maline veiling misty over full-blown roses. Open crown. Rich-looking straw-like cloth.

$2.48 — GLAMOUR CALOT. Your hair shines through leaf-circle design. Wonderful straw braid stitched to look like embroidery. Dotted border rayon veil.

$3.34 — HALO OF RUSTLY RAYON TAFFETA loops in back of flattering roll brim. Dressy straw-like cloth, open crown. Elastic back adjusts to fit you perfectly.

$2.29 — PERT POSTILLION with smart side interest. Rayon taffeta loops, scalloped cuff brim. Self-covered loop at back. Shiny straw-like braid.

$3.29 — DASHING SELF-BOW adds drama to dress hat of glistening cellophane braid. Full crown fits comfortably.

$3.59 — SOFTLY ROUNDED off-the-face bumper has big dressmaker bow of rayon taffeta at back. Fine straw braid.

$3.98 — FINE STRAW BRAID SCOTTY with lovely cluster of hyacinths.

(A) Lacy wide scallop brim with open crown; (B) Wider Side look drape pleated above the brow; Row (2) Felt Disc with lot of flowers; Sweetheart Bonnet with roses and an open crown; Leaf circle design Calot with full veil; Halo with roll brim and open crown; (3) Postillion with Taffeta loops at side; Cellophane braid with large self bow; Off-the-face Bumper with full back bow; Straw braid Scotty with hyacinth cluster. 1949 Sears, Roebuck and Co. catalog for Spring and Summer.

$1.98 $2.59 $2.98

$3.49

BEWITCHING picture hat. Row-on-row bands of sheer braid and felt (70% wool, 30% cotton). Big bow in front.

STRAW BRAID.

OFF-THE-FACE brim dips at side. Big lovely rayon taffeta bow. Open crown. Straw-like braid.

WHITE ROSES nestle beneath curve of Watteau brim. Straw braid.

$1.98 $2.29 $2.19 $2.37 $1.68

SHINING METAL THREADS crocheted with straw-like braid. Open crown.

RUFFLED HALO. Rows of shirred rayon taffeta. Sheer braid half hat clips on head snugly.

STRAW-LIKE BRAID.

SWEETHEART BONNET, frilly maline ruffles. Open crown. Straw braid.

CUTE CALOT crocheted of fine straw-like braid, hugs the head. Two self-covered pins.

$1.98 $2.98 $1.98 $1.79 $2.34

RICH STRAW-LIKE CLOTH bumper sits high on your forehead. Grosgrain ribbon circles open crown. Trim back bow.

SMART SAILOR has straw-edged rayon taffeta rosette, graceful quill. Elastic headsize band. Straw braid.

DEEP CROWN CLASSIC with posey at side. Straw braid.

SOFTLY TURNED-DOWN BRIM, dashing cockade of pleated grosgrain ribbon. Straw braid.

PRETTY POSTILLION has smart new crown, big back bow of rayon taffeta ribbon. Straw-like braid.

(A) Row on row sheer braid band Picture with open crown; (B) Straw braid; (C) Off-the-face brim dips at side; (D) Watteau brim with roses beneath a curve; Row (2) Metallic crochet with open crown; Shirred taffeta ruffled Halo; Straw like braid; Sweetheart Bonnet with ruffles to adorn the open crown; Crocheted Calot; (3) Straw cloth Bumper with open crown; Sailor with taffeta rosette; Deep crown Classic with posey at side; Turned down brim with pleated ribbon cockade; Postillion with back bow. 1949 Sears, Roebuck and Co. catalog for Spring and Summer.

(A) Flowered Bumper; (B) Straw braid Homburg; (C) Straw braid Profile Beret; Row (2) Straw braid with nosegay; Bloused crown Sailor; Straw-like braid Bumper with flowers and bow; Modified Tricorne with taffeta flowers; (3) Felt Classic Casual; Sailor with taffeta ribbon cascade; Straw-like braid with huge pearl-like pin; Straw braid Beret with taffeta bows. 1949 Sears, Roebuck and Co. catalog for Spring and Summer.

FLOWERED BUMPER. Straw-like braid.

SOFTLY FEMININE STRAW-BRAID HOMBURG.

PROFILE BERET. Straw braid.

$2.34 $3.59 $3.69

$3.29 $2.39 $2.59 $3.94

NOSEGAY CHARMER with flattering lines. Smooth straw braid.

LUSCIOUS FLOWER, sheer braid bows are eye-catchers on bloused-crown sailor. Straw-like braid.

DRESSY STRAW-LIKE BRAID BUMPER is lavishly flowered, has loop in back that assures perfect fit.

TRIM MODIFIED TRICORNE accented with a cluster of rayon taffeta flowers, grosgrain ribbon. Straw braid.

$2.49 $3.98 $1.98 $3.98

CLASSIC CASUAL, novelty stitching. Soft-dip brim, upturned back. Crown is self-laced. Fine wool felt.

BERIBBONED SAILOR. Rippling cascade of shirred rayon taffeta ribbon flares smartly at side. Finely woven straw.

TAILORED CLASSIC in straw-like braid has smart pearl-like pin, loops of grosgrain ribbon at sides.

STRIKING NEW BERET. Fine quality straw braid, softly indented, with rich rayon taffeta bows.

(A) Off-the-face Profile with ostrich plume curl; (B) Felt Breton with round crown and creased brim with feather trim; (C) Unusual feather umbrella brim. 1949 Montgomery Ward catalog for Fall and Winter.

Foremost Silhouettes

ROMANTIC OFF-THE-FACE PROFILE HAT

A A curl of feather and a mist of veiling lend this Hat a romantic air. Deftly designed of supple New Wool Felt on head-hugging lines that complement your hair-do. The side-slanting angle and coquettish, natural color Ostrich plume becomes most any age—flatter a pretty profile. Finished with tiny felt bow; veil.

SMART CLOSE FITTING BRETON

B Fashioned of a finer quality New Wool Felt with a smooth finish. Its round crown and circular creased brim have a becomingly youthful air. Its tailored simplicity is accented by a single saucy "brush" of rich, silky feathers. Distinctively detailed with Grosgrain tubing band and a swirl of flattering mesh veiling. Ideal for Fall Suits now and Winter wear later.

DRAMATIC "UMBRELLA" FEATHER BRIM HAT

C Unusually designed to give you a Hat of true distinction and lavishly trimmed to keep you in step with the new elegance of feminine Fall fashions. Sleek shiny feathers frame your face with soft flattery—add drama to any outfit. The crown and underbrim are luxuriously detailed in Rayon Velvet.

HOW TO MEASURE FOR HATS

Measure your head size as shown in the sketch. The number of inches shown on tape is your actual head size. All hats do not come in all sizes. Make sure that the hat you wish to order is listed in size you require.

(A) Felt Profile Beret with feather wings; (B) Felt high crown Cloche with feathers; (C) Felt Breton covered with feathers; (D) Off-the-face Breton with ostrich plume; (E) Sailor with satin rosette; (F) Felt Suiter with feather stick-up; (G) Felt Casual with feather cluster; (H) Felt Suiter with back Satin bow; (J) Felt Casual with telescope crown; (K) Off-the-face tilted Profile; (L) Suiter with sequined band and large back bow. 1949 Montgomery Ward catalog for Fall and Winter.

Women's Fall Styles

A PROFILE BERET of good New Wool Felt. Smartly trimmed with rich feather wings.

B HIGH CROWN CLOCHE of good New Wool Felt attractively trimmed with lustrous feathers and soft mesh veil.

C DRAMATIC BRETON of finer quality New Wool Felt with lustrous silky feathers.

D OFF THE FACE BRETON of good New Wool Felt. Fluffy Ostrich plume, mesh veil.

E DRESSY SAILOR of good New Wool Felt. Shirred Rayon Satin rosette and band, mesh veil.

F DRESSY SUITER of good New Wool Felt. Smart feather "stick-up," mesh veil. Rayon Satin trim.

G FEATHER TRIMMED CASUAL for the more mature woman. Of New Wool Felt with feather cluster.

H CLASSIC SUITER of New Wool Felt with mesh veil overlay and back bow of Rayon Satin. Colors.

J TELESCOPE CROWN CASUAL of good New Wool Felt. Smartly trimmed with nailhead ornaments set in Grosgrain band.

K OFF THE FACE PROFILE HAT of New Wool Felt. Colorful ornament and mesh veil dress up this flattering style.

L SEQUIN TRIMMED SUITER of New Wool Felt. Rayon Satin bow and veil accent smartly tailored lines.

Profusely Trimmed

(L) **Provocative Profile Beret** dips low on one side, sweeps high on the other. In good New Wool Felt with Grosgrain ribbon bow nestled in front. Soft mesh veil.

(M) **Cushion Brim Toque** in better New Wool Felt. Matching double feather "stick-up" rises from the creased brim. Trim felt band ends in a pretty bow in back.

(N) **Dressy-off-the-face Bonnet** radiates quiet charm. Of better New Wool Felt. Lustrous Rayon Velvet faces underbrim, forms band. Matching feather cluster.

(P) **Sophisticated Dressy Bonnet** of good New Wool Felt. Becoming off-the-face style flatteringly detailed with bows of swishy-crisp Rayon Taffeta. Trim felt band.

(R) **Creased-Crown Pillbox** has round young lines and a youthful air. Simply styled in New Wool Felt with a natural color quill. A shiny bow of Rayon Satin tubing, a swirling mesh veil add softness.

(T) **Off-the-Face Profile Hat** styled with drama in good New Wool Felt. Distinctively trimmed with a feminine bow and streamers in back of shiny Rayon Satin; mesh veil.

(U) **Hand-draped and Tucked Turban** is always flattering, always smart and wonderfully becoming. In lustrous Rayon Velvet.

(V) **Feather Trimmed Suiter** in New Wool Felt. Distinctively styled in a feminine version of a gentleman's Homburg. Feather "stick-up", Grosgrain ribbon band.

(W) **The Cushion Brim Bumper** molded gently to your head in New Wool Felt. Glittering band of sequins, Grosgrain back bow.

(X) **Off-the-Face Profile Hat** styled to attract compliments, in New Wool Felt. Tastefully trimmed with Rayon Satin bow loops. A swirl of soft mesh veil adds charm.

(L) Profile Beret with side dip; (M) Cushion brim Toque with double feather stick-up; (N) Off-the-face Bonnet with feather cluster; (P) Felt Bonnet with Taffeta bows; (R) Felt creased crown Pillbox with veil; (T) Off-the-face Profile with bow and streamers in back; (U) Velvet draped and tucked Turban; (V) Feather trimmed Suiter Homburg; (W) Molded cushion brim Bumper; (X) Off-the-face Profile with satin bow loops. 1949 Montgomery Ward catalog for Fall and Winter.

Beautifully Trimmed

PRETTY RIPPLE BRIM BONNET

(D) This bonny little Bonnet is artfully styled to be pretty as well as smart. The round lines of the soft New Wool Felt crown and the bow loops of lustrous Rayon Satin emphasize its air of sweet femininity. The side-dipping brim gives it just the right touch of sophistication for smartness. Swirling mesh veil.

FEATHER TRIMMED OFF-THE-FACE HAT

(E) The smart, head-hugging lines of this Hat reflect the foremost trends of Fashion . . . show off your hair-do. Simply styled in fine quality New Wool Felt. A colorful feather bird perches on the brim, spreads its wings skywards. Tastefully trimmed with crisp Rayon Taffeta tubing band on brim.

DASHING BERET CROWN CLOCHE

(F) A Hat that's twice as smart as most because it cleverly combines two styles. Ingeniously designed in a fine quality, smooth and supple New Wool Felt. The beret crown is draped smartly above a rolled brim entirely covered in rich harmonizing Rayon Velvet. A twin "brush" of fashionable silky feathers.

(D) Ripple brim Bonnet with crown bow loops; (E) Felt with a feather bird perched on the brim; (F) Felt Beret crown Cloche with a feather brush. 1949 Montgomery Ward catalog for Fall and Winter.

CHAPTER 5: 1950 TO 1959

(A) Flower trimmed Capulet in felt; (B) Felt Derby with feather brush; (C) Crocheted Off-the-face with French knot trim; (D) Off-the-face Profile with huge petal flower trim; (E) Velvet cuffed Helmet. 1951-52 Montgomery Ward catalog for Fall and Winter.

(N) Ripple scoop Bonnet with felt covered button to accent each ripple; (P) Felt Profile Off-the-face with feather and cord whip trim; (R) Feathered Pillbox; (T) Fur felt Tyrolean; (U) Felt Off-the-face with quill and feathers. 1951-52 Montgomery Ward catalog for Fall and Winter.

(T) Velvet Helmet with feather pinwheel; (U) Glitter banded Cloche; (V) Six-section crown Crew with snap brim; (W) Felt cushion brim Toque with fancy feathers and veil; (X) Felt Profile Beret with quill trim; (Y) Cushion brim Cloche with bow and streamer trim; (Z) Wool knit Helmet with a tassel and a bicycle clip to keep it securely on the head. 1951-52 Montgomery Ward catalog for Fall and Winter.

 (U) Fur felt Off-the-face with pleated ribbon cocarde; (V) Velvet button bordered Helmet; (W) Velvet with visor brim and mock pearls; (X) Profile Toque with pleated ribbon cocarde; (Y) Velvet Pillbox with self covered buttons; (Z) Wedding ring Toque with quill and tiny flowers. 1951-52 Montgomery Ward catalog for Fall and Winter.

(D) Parisian Suiter with wings springing from a cocarde; (E) Velvet Profile with feather and veil; (F) All feather Capulet; (G) Triple tiered Toque; (H) Off-the-face Profile with ribbon cocarde; (J) Casual Scarf-hat with rolled brim; (K) Crocheted chenille Off-the-face. 1951-52 Montgomery Ward catalog for Fall and Winter.

Paris says *Lovely Violets*

① 4.98

Paris says *Sweet Peas*

② 2.49

Paris says *Dainty Daisies*

③ 3.98

Paris says *Flowers*

④ 4.69
Velvet or Pique

⑤ 2.49

⑥ 2.49

⑦ 2.49

SHELL BONNETS in Pique, Straw Cloth, or Velvet!

3 new versions of the biggest hat hit from coast to coast!
Every inch feminine—becoming to every woman under the sun!
And each style in your choice of 3 fashion-wise fabrics!

2.49 EACH   ANY **2** for **4.75**

NEWEST BACK LOOK!

Flower-decked—so very new "coming and going"!

⑧ 3.49

⑨ 3.49

⑩ 2.69

(1) Straw cloth completely covered in flowers; Straw cloth with deep fit crown and filmy veil; (3) Daisy covered Helmet; (4) Daisy banded with net crown; (5) Button rimmed Shell Bonnet; (6) Scalloped Shell Bonnet; (7) Rhinestone studded scalloped Shell Bonnet; (8) Straw Rocker Bonnet with back flowers and bow; (9) Velvet banded and bowed straw Bonnet; (10) Big side and back brim with daisy strewn halo. 1952 Aldens catalog for Spring and Summer.

Row (1) Triple-tier Coolie; Button-top Coolie; Feather Bonnet; Side sweep feather Half hat; Off-the-face Profile; (2) Velvet birds perched on a bow; Head hugging straw with contrast piping; Off-the-face candy straw with feather; Straw with two large feathers; (3) Sailor with grosgrain band; Sailor with floral band; Feather Helmet; Swiss straw Profile; Feather pinwheel on Half hat. 1952 Aldens catalog for Spring and Summer.

Row (1) Tie on Veil; Blossom tie on Veil; Flowered spray Pillbox; Button topped straw cloth Pillbox; Velvet trim felt Pillbox; (2) Posey wreathed half hat; Halo half hat; Veiled Helmet; Lace inset back in straw cloth; (3) Straw cloth with posey visor and lacy crown; Daisy cap with rayon net crown and peek-a-boo veil; Fur felt Helmet with felt daisies; Helmet with pointed brim; Bustle-back Helmet. 1952 Aldens catalog for Spring and Summer.

Row (1) Straw and felt with swagger brim; (2) Anglo-basque Beret; Ripple crown Beret; Lacy shadow brim with cut out crown; Cartwheel with mesh veiled crown drifting to ties; Straw braid ripple brim; (3) Straw braid visor with velvet band; Felt visor with button trim; Starched lace Profile with contrast brim; Lacy coronet Halo; Wedding ring with lace crown. 1952 Aldens catalog for Spring and Summer.

Row (1) Veiling over open crown Roller; Peaked Visor; Straw cloth with daisy halo; Draped faille with bonnet brim; (2) Square Scoop Bonnet with veil; Straw cloth Wedding Ring; Helmet with umbrella feather; Cloche Bonnet; (3) Floral Half hat; Side pleated Profile; Off-the-face Roller; Straw cloth with iridescent brim and flowing veil. 1952 Aldens catalog for Spring and Summer.

Top row left to right: Colonial Breton; Flowered profile Toque; Cushion-brim suiter; Flower wreathed Sailor (2) Off-the-face with a wreath of Spring flowers; Profile Toque of shiny straw; Profile Toque with grosgrain band swirls; Notched-brim Sailor (3) Synthetic straw cloth Profile; "Wedding ring" Calot; Pedaline Braid profile Beret; Peaked Sailor with white lilacs and leaves. 1953 Montgomery Ward Catalog for Spring and Summer.

Crocheted Coolie Hat and matching bag. 1953 Hand Crochet Fashions by Dritz.

Crocheted Pixie Hat and matching pouch bag. 1953 Hand Crochet Fashions by Dritz.

Crocheted Hat with bead trim and matching handbag. 1953 Hand Crochet Fashions by Dritz.

Top row, left to right: Feminine mushroom Bonnet with flock-dot veiling; Large brimmed straw Classic; Picture hat designed to frame the face; (2) graceful Cloche Bonnet with a floral wreath; Toyo cloth scoop shell Bonnet; Sprays of lilacs on a rocker Bonnet; Straw "puritan" bonnet; (3) "Sugar scoop" shell Bonnet; Lifted-brim straw Bonnet; Cloche Bonnet with halo of pleated grosgrain; Flower-wreathed Bonnet. 1953 Montgomery Ward catalog for Spring and Summer.

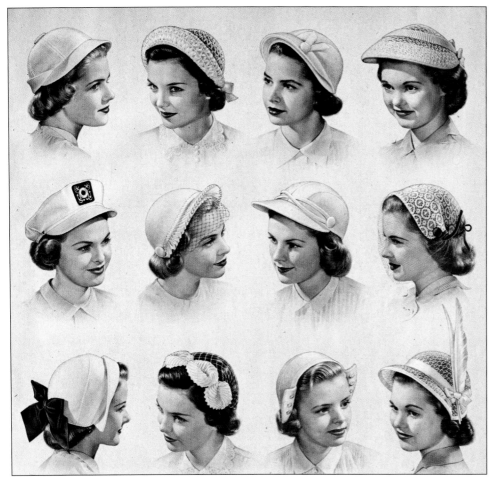

Top row, left to right: Popular "Chukker" style in cotton pique; Off-the-face traveler retains its shape even after packing; Lifted brim Cloche; Lacy textured "Coolie" hat; (2) Spritely "Skipper" cap; Pleated brim Bonnet; Jaunty Jockey cap; Cotton lace pinched Capulet; (3) Cotton pique Off-the-face; Cocarde Capulet; Cotton pique Dutch Bonnet; Textured cotton boucle Cloche Bonnet. 1953 Montgomery Ward catalog for Spring and Summer.

Top row, left to right: Double cushion brim Bonnet; Ripple brim Sailor with white cotton lace medallions over a velvet band; Profile Beret with texture and color contrast; Plateau Shell; (2) Square Shell Bonnet; Side bowed Profile Beret; Every popular big brimmed Classic; Smartly-styled cushion brim Toque; (3) Handsome dressy Homburg; Softly curved Off-the-face Profile; Straw cushion brim Cloche with Spring flower wreath; Simple creased crown Cloche. 1953 Montgomery Ward catalog for Spring and Summer.

Top row, left to right: Flower peaked Shell Bonnet; Ripple brim Plateau with lilac sprays; Two-tone draped Profile; Flowered Bonnet laden with Spring flowers (2) Off-the-face Profile; Off-the-face Profile with a sweeping rolled brim; Draped Profile; Draped Toque with a sprightly floral stick-up (3) Flowered straw Profile Beret; Deftly draped Toque; Profile Beret with gay flower cluster; Cotton lace Off-the-face Profile topped with a velvet flower. 1953 Montgomery Ward catalog for Spring and Summer.

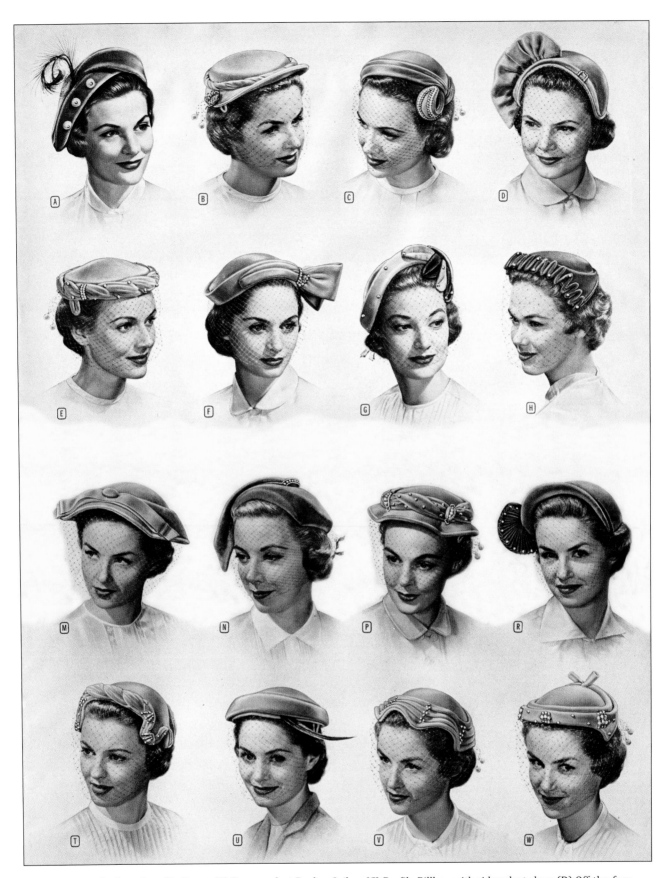

(A) Side swept feathered profile Beret; (B) Rayon velvet Rocker Sailor; (C) Profile Pillbox with side velvet claw; (D) Off-the-face Capulet with side shirred velvet fan; (E) Draped Pillbox with mock pearls; (F) Bowed Pillbox with side bow loop; (G) Petal leaf Profile; (H) Cuffed Shell sprinkled with rhinestones; (J) Side rose Profile; (K) Velvet drape Pillbox with piercing quill; (L) Beehive Cloche; (M) rippled brim Bonnet; (Q) Dramatic winged Pillbox in velvet; (P) Velvet rippled brim Sailor; (R) Charming velvet Off-the-face Bonnet; (T) Small and glamorous jeweled "clutch" Shell; (U) Smartly tailored feathered Shell; (V) Tucked Shell Bonnet with a rippling brim; (W) Meweled "clutch" Toque fits closely to the head. 1955-56 Montgomery Ward catalog for Fall and Winter.

(A) Profile Scoop with pheasant feather; (B) Ribbon trimmed Plateau with tie back veil; (C) Clutch Shell with tie back veil; (D) Off-the-face bowed Toque with rhinestones and mock pearls; (E) Profile Beret with crystal beaded ornaments and rhinestones; (F) Velour Coolie with bugle beads; (G) Profile with beaded leaf motif; (H) Felt Cloche with tri-color band; (J) Felt Beret with edge cording; (K) Tiered Profile Toque with rhinestones; (L) Wide brimmed Sailor with jewel ornaments; (M) Jewel sparked Pillbox; (N) Wool felt quilled Suiter; (P) Lifted brim Bonnet of brushed felt; (R) Beaded triple-tier Shetl; (T) Fanciful Sailor with lavish rhinestone trim; (U) Beehive Cloche with a slender felt band; (V) Feathered Shell Bonnet; Face framing Cloche Bonnet. 1955-56 Montgomery Ward catalog for Fall and Winter.

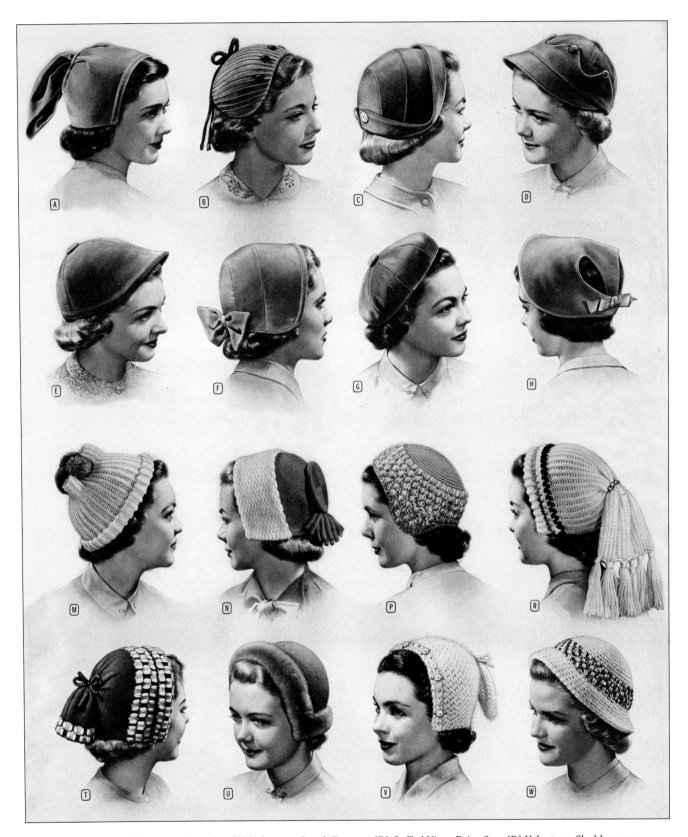

(A) Ponytail Helmet; (B) Tucked Capulet; (C) Velveteen Dutch Bonnet; (D) Cuffed Visor Brim Cap; (D) Velveteen Chukker cap; (F) Head-hugging bowed Helmet; (G) Velveteen Beret; (H) Velveteen Cloche Bonnet; (M) Shako turban of wool double knit rib stitch; (N) Head hugging Helmet with tassel; (P) Hand-crocheted Halo Helmet; (R) "Pony tail" cap; (T) "Pony tail" clip cap with hidden head clip for secure fit; (U) Mouton trimmed clip Cap; (V) Jeweled "Pony Tail" cap, (W) Wool crocheted Cloche. 1955-56 Montgomery Ward catalog for Fall and Winter.

(X) Velvet Capulet with mock pearls and cording; (Y) Velvet Cuffed Pillbox with a Satin rosette; (Z) Scoop Bonnet encircled with an accent of twisted Velvet; (J) Velvet Profile with side rose; (K) Velvet Pillbox with piercing quill; (L) Beehive Cloche with bow and feather trim. 1955-56 Montgomery Ward catalog for Fall and Winter.

(A) Hand-crocheted Helmet with petal topknot; (B) Dome Pillbox with attached scarf; (C) Cuddle Cap with sham pearls; (D) Angora Beanie; (E) Hand-crocheted Halo Cap with loop fringe crown; (F) Popcorn stitch crochet with back tassel; (G) Front bandeau clip on Helmet with Pompon; (H) Male inspired Ivy League Cap; (J) Classic Cloche; (K) Beaded Helmet with back bow; (L) Ponytail Helmet with make-believe pearls; (M) Tie on Headband. 1956 Sears, Roebuck and Co. catalog for Fall and Winter.

CASUAL CAPS ARE FUN TO WEAR

A Pert Petal Topknot accented with dewdrop make-believe pearls makes this hand-crocheted all wool bonnet a perfect charmer for fall and winter.

B The Dome Pillbox in wool jersey is all set for winter winds and cold with its attached scarf. Ties under chin.

C Dressed-up Cuddle Cap with a generous sprinkling of sham pearls for all-out flattery. Fits all head sizes.

D Kitten-Soft Beanie for the young at heart. Made of the fluffiest combination of 30% wool, 70% angora rabbit hair, 100% cotton backing. Eight-section crown with top loop. Your favorite for fall and winter.

E Exquisitely Hand-Crocheted Halo Cap in 100% wool. Loop fringe crown glistens with many tiny harmonizing beads. Notice the saucy back bow.

F Pert Top and Brim in a carefully hand-crocheted popcorn stitch on a cozy and warm 100% wool hat. Tassel back adds a note of cheer.

G A Fluffy-Soft Pompon sits right at the back of a 60% wool, 20% angora rabbit hair and 20% nylon helmet. Front bandeau clip.

H Ivy League Cap, just like a college boy's for the newest look this season. Visored wool jersey, looks so authentic with its back buckle and belt.

J The Classic Cloche teams up smartly with all your suits and coats.

K Saucy Bow at the back of a beaded helmet for a feminine flourish. Fits snugly with front bandeau clip.

L Popular Ponytail Helmet showered with make-believe pearls. Snug bandeau clip at front. Fits all head sizes.

M Bewitching Headband hugs your head snugly, keeps your ears warm with the perfect combination of 40% wool, 30% angora rabbit hair and 30% nylon.

(A) Velvet with large brim; (B)Velvet Shell with quills; (C) Velvet with self draped edge; (D) Velvet with bugle beads and faux pearls; (E) Satin shirring circles a rayon velvet Shell; (F) Velvet Sailor; (G) Velvet Profile with feathers; (H) Rayon satin shirred Pillbox; (J) Squared Shell with bugle beads; (K) Velvet Tambourine; (L) Shirred Rayon velvet with feather; (M) Panne Rayon velvet with shirring all around. 1956 Sears, Roebuck and Co. catalog for Fall and Winter.

GLAMOROUS HEADLINE FASHIONS

A LARGE-BRIMMED BEAUTY for eye-shadowing flattery. Smooth rayon velvet bound with grosgrain. Graceful bow of tubular grosgrain ribbon at center.

B JAUNTY SHELL of lustrous rayon velvet with two smart quills for the dramatic accent every woman loves. Crisp tie-back rayon veil.

C DEEP IN FASHION. Flattering rayon velvet with self-draped edge. Grosgrain trim and bow. Rich rhinestone ornament.

D LEAFY CONFECTION frames a pretty face in soft rayon velvet, showered with gleaming bugle beads and make-believe pearls. Tie-back rayon veil.

E SLEEK RAYON SATIN SHIRRING circles the rayon velvet shell in soft folds. Pert stick-up tab subtly touched with sham pearl motif. Tie-back rayon veil.

F INTERESTING SAILOR STYLE in rayon velvet with an exciting feather fancy. Twisted, pleated rayon satin circles crown. Rayon veil.

G FANCIFUL FEATHERS with an elegant sweep on a rayon velvet profiler for maximum fashion. Rayon veil.

H FEMININE SOPHISTICATION. Glowing rayon satin pillbox, softly shirred, trimmed with sham pearl and bead ornament. Tie-back rayon veil.

J GLAMOUR GALORE for the season's most festive occasions. A flattering squared shell, covered with bugle beads and shell-like accents. Crisp rayon veil.

K THE EXCITING TAMBOURINE in rayon velvet does wonderful things for you. Rayon satin ribbon around brim, accented with rhinestone ornaments. Rayon veil.

L THE SPIRIT OF FASHION expressed in a softly shirred rayon velvet hat, cleverly accented with a feather fancy. Tie-back rayon veil, covered clips.

M THE SHAPE TO SHOUT ABOUT in precious Panné rayon velvet with graceful shirring all around. Flashed with two sparkling rhinestone ornaments.

BUDGET PRICED BEAUTIES

• styled for feminine flattery
in precious rayon velvet $2.98 EACH

A FESTIVE CALOT, showered with sequins, trimmed with little bows. Dress-up rayon velvet makes you look lovely for many a memorable occasion. The little hat every woman needs.

B SWEETHEART CAP, gently shaped for all-out flattery. Drapery drama in pleated rayon grosgrain on rayon velvet shell, creates this captivating charmer for a pretty lady.

C CHARMING FASHION. Swirling scrolls prettily circle this rayon velvet charmer, adorned with lustrous sham pearls strategically placed. Wonderful for special occasions. Rayon veil.

D LUSTROUS RAYON VELVET PILLBOX with shimmering rayon satin twist all around. Stunning rhinestone ornament, attention-getting feather. Rayon velvet covered side clips. Rayon veil.

E RAYON SATIN TUBING across top of pillbox bumper ends in side clips. Stunning rayon plush velvet accented with a pretty rhinestone and jaunty feather. Tie-back rayon veil.

F GLEAMING RAYON SATIN DRAPE softly frames rayon velvet helmet. Flashed with fiery rhinestone and sham pearls. Dress-up beauty for every occasion. Romantic rayon veil.

G PRETTY TURN-UP BRIM ends in saucy side bow. Rayon velvet profiler gaily accented with feather spray. Make it your basic favorite for fall and winter.

H CASCADE OF GLAMOROUS FEATHERS on one side of rayon velvet pillbox. Gleaming rayon satin insert makes for added flattery. Sequins accent feathers. Romantic rayon veil.

J THE NEW BULKY LOOK. You'll be in step with the latest fashion when you wear this beautifully shaped dome in glowing rayon velvet. Subtly accented with sparkling rhinestones. Rayon veil.

K SOPHISTICATED RAYON SATIN DRAPE circles the sweet rayon velvet shell. Fanciful clipped feather gaily curls on this winning charmer. Rayon velvet covered side clips. Rayon veil.

L ENCHANTING GARLANDS fashioned for feminine flattery. Delicate pressed rayon velvet leaves alive with gleaming rhinestones to make you look totally wonderful. A fitting climax for pretty outfits. Rayon veil.

M SHIRRED DRAMA on brim makes this rayon velvet a beauty from every angle. A big-brimmed hat superbly designed to flatter. Scheduled for big occasions all fall and winter. Tie-back rayon veil for a lovely illusion.

(A) Calot with sequins; (B) Sweetheart Cap with pleated ribbon trim; (C) Velvet scrolls with sham pearls; (D) Velvet Pillbox with a satin twist all around; (E) Pillbox with satin tubing across the top; (F) Satin drape Helmet with rhinestones and sham pearls; (G) Profiler with turn-up brim; (H) Pillbox with side feathers; (J) Velvet Dome with rhinestones and veil; (K) Satin drape circles the velvet Shell; (L) Pressed velvet leaves with a veil; (M) Velvet with big shirred brim. 1956 Sears, Roebuck and Co. catalog for Fall and Winter.

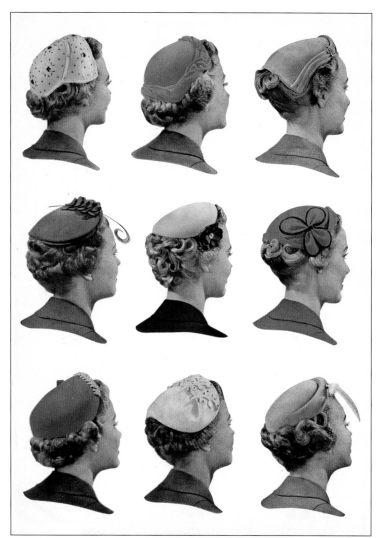

Row (1) Head hugging glitter enhanced Shell; Draped Turban Toque; Self corded Shell (2) Miniature Beret with petals pierced by a feather; Veiled miniature Beret dotted with rhinestones; Bowed Rocker Bonnet with bows on each side; (3) Velour Pillbox jeweled with glitter ornaments and mock pearls; Leaf Capulet with rhinestones and pearls and a tie back veil; Velour Toque with feather strands out one side. 1955-56 Montgomery Ward catalog for Fall and Winter.

(A) Straw with dimpled curve; (B) Straw look cloth Shell with feather trim; (C) Shell with ripple front; (D) Peaked Shell with tie-back veil; (G) Curled feather cap; (H) Straw braid Scoop Bonnet with draping; (J) Veiled Scoop Bonnet; (K) Beehive with velvet bows; (N) Straw look cloth Shell with pearls and flowers; (P) Veiled Sweetheart Shell; (R) Straw Scoop with chiffon roses; (S) Sculptured cotton lace Shell; (V) Split-brim Profile Bonnet; (W) Sailor with floral wreath; (X) Straw with cushion brim; (Y) Straw like cloth Shell with sequins. 1956 Sears, Roebuck and Co. catalog for Spring and Summer.

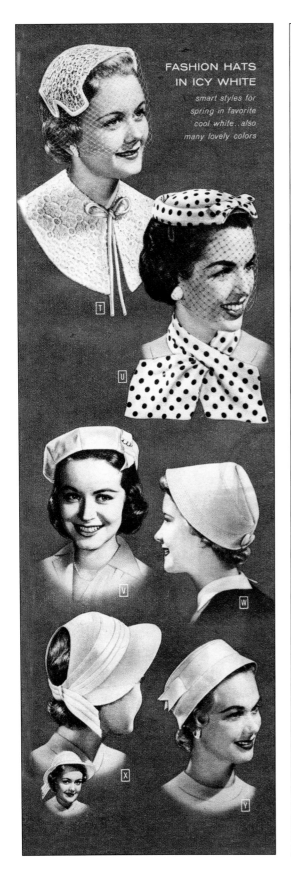

(T) Puritan style Cap and collar set; (U) V-front Pillbox in polka dot fabric; (V) Beret with sham pearls and simulated jewels; (W) Dutch style Cloche; (X) Face framing Bonnet of linen look rayon; (Y) Rayon Coachman Cloche. 1956 Sears, Roebuck and Co. catalog for Spring and Summer.

(E) Straw look cloth Skimmer Portrait; (F) Claw Cap with Rayon lilacs and rhinestones; (L) Ripple brim with flowers; (M) Pleated Rayon taffeta Pillbox with sham pearls; (T) Veiled triple brim Shell; (U) Calot with bows; (Z) Linen-look rayon Portrait; (AA) Molded Plateau with draped rayon veiling. 1956 Sears, Roebuck and Co. catalog for Spring and Summer.

(F) Nylon knit head warmer; (G) Nylon square scarf with hand rolled edges; (H) Royal Stewart clan plaid head warmer; (J) Acrilan jersey Cuddle Cap with pearl nailheads; (K) Dacron headsquare with all around self fringe; (L) Nylon Ascot Hood; (M) Crusader style Helmet of Acrilan jersey; (N) Acrilan jersey Ascot Hood with wool crochet trim. 1956 Sears, Roebuck and Co. catalog for Fall and Winter.

(A) Petal Helmet; (B) Lattice Cap with rhinestones; (C) Forward Shell with wreath of flowers; (D) Helmet with peek-a-boo back; (E) Draped tiers with rosebud trim; (F) Straw effect cloth with wreath of flowers; (G) Off-the-face Pillbox; (H) Straw look cloth in a Halo Bandeau; (J) Straw braid rippled Beret; (K) Straw braid with appliqued leaves; (L) Side swept Profile; (M) Cloth bonnet with self drape edges; (N) Off-the-face Profile with roll back brim; (P) Straw braid Sailor; (R) Straw braid with Plateau brim; (S) Two-tone straw braid Bonnet. 1956 Sears, Roebuck and Co. catalog for Spring and Summer.

Genuine Beaver Fur Felts

Captivating Styles . . . All Beautiful and Excitingly New

ADD THE CROWNING TOUCH TO ALL YOUR COSTUMES

$5.98 AND $7.98

BEAUTIFULLY STYLED WOOLS, VELVETS AND FEATHERS

(A) Fur felt Profile with pheasant feather; (B) Long nap beaver fur felt Draped Beret; (C) Long nap beaver fur felt rippled brim Cloche. 1958-59 Montgomery Ward catalog for Fall and Winter.

(D) Felt draped Profile Turban with mesh veil; (E) Pillbox with Rayon Satin bow and band; (F) Velvet draped Off-the-face Toque with rhinestones; (G) Velvet draped Turban with rhinestones and mesh veil; (H) Dainty Shell with feathers; (J) Cloche with swirling hackle feathers in front; (K) Profile Beret with rayon satin bow; (L) Draped Snood Beret adorned with metallic nail head beads. 1958-59 Montgomery Ward catalog for Fall and Winter.

Row (1) Large floral brim and open net crown; Braid brim with organza crown; Petal Cloche; Braid brim with taffeta draped crown; (2) Fluffy braided tulle; Lilies of the Valley Cap; (3) Floral Pixie Pillbox; Swirled rosette crown; Demi-Cap with curled feathers; Carnation Halo with net crown. 1962 Sears, Roebuck and Co. catalog for Spring and Summer.

Exquisite Bloom, a single glorious rose perched at a tantilizing angle on a chenille-dotted veil.

Curling Feathers and rayon satin leaves nestle together on an easy-to-wear pillbox. Veil.

Draped Veiling shapes the brim of this cloche for a dramatic and very becoming effect. Textured braid crown.

Slant on Spring is all rosy when you wear this lovely profile hat . . enchanting rose cluster and petals of rayon organza.

Fluffy Flattery, a delicious concoction of soft feathers. Rayon velvet bow nestles in front.

Blossoming Roses as light and colorful as Spring itself. Rayon organza roses and net.

SMART

Sculptured Pillbox. Pleats of rayon organza; rayon velvet trim. Open crown.

Flowery Scoop. Heaps of beautiful carnations on a ripple-brim cloche.

Glamorous Turban drapes beautifully above your brow. Shaped of nylon tulle, accented with rayon velvet.

Berry Buds cap your head in a spritely fashion. Rayon satin leaf crown.

Row (1) A single fabric rose to cover the head with an attached veil; Curled feather Pillbox; Cloche with draped veiling brim; Profile with rose cluster; (2) Soft feathers with velvet bow; Organza roses and net; (3) Pleated organza Pillbox; Floral covered ripple brim Cloche; Draped tulle Turban; Half-hat with berry buds. 1962 Sears, Roebuck and Co. catalog for Spring and Summer.

Row (1) Cloche with double roses; Rough braid Breton; Floral Toque; Brow tipping cross tab Beret; Dome silhouette Pillbox; (2) Button top Cloche; Organza with floppy brim; Shirred organza; Net wrapped Cloche; (3) Boutonniere Pillbox; Bonnet with crown of carnations; Veiled Derby. 1962 Sears, Roebuck and Co. catalog for Spring and Summer.

Romantic Roses side by side on cloche that looks like straw.

Brim Up . . rough-textured braid breton rolls merrily through spring and summer. Band.

Blossom Out in a flowered toque paved with sweet peas. Dotted veil top; face veil.

Parisian Flavor . . saucy beret with brow-tipping cross-tabs of rayon satin. Soft but crisp straw-like cloth.

Shape and Texture, a dome silhouette pillbox . . textured to look like straw. Circlet of white lilies on the crown.

[1] Enchantingly Demure . . button-top cloche of rayon organza with rayon velvet.

[2] Sheer Froth whipped of rayon organza. Floppy brim, plush rayon velvet trim.

[3] Soft and Alluring, shirred rayon organza over rayon taffeta.

[4] Glamorous Swath of net wrapped around a rising cloche. Glittering butterfly bow.

White "Boutonniere" Buds look so dainty on shaped pillbox that looks like straw. Veil.

Spring Bonnet looks like straw, fills its crown with carnations. Veil.

Dashing Derby of perido straw. Wide rayon taffeta band. Veil.

Profile Cloche . . textured to look like straw. Deepened crown, side dipping brim. Rayon organza band on crown.

Flower Top, a crownful of blossoms on this wavy-brimmed cloche of rustic braid.

Envelope Pillbox sealed with a flat bow of rayon grosgrain. Crisp Perido straw; wisp veil.

Textured Straw-look Beret, easy-to-wear, quick-to-flatter. Cuffed with white lilies.

High Crown, Deepened Brim straw with a 2-tone bow.

[1] Dramatic Bouffant, a provocative shape of softly rippled and shirred acetate taffeta. Double fabric brim dips in profile slant.

[2] Wide-brimmed Picture Hat for a garden party look with sheers and summery cottons. Cut-out crown. Perido straw trimmed with self band.

[3] Swirls of Organza (rayon) spin around this petite pillbox. Rayon velvet cuff.

[4] Sitting Pretty on the back of your head, a little pillbox in a crisp fabric that looks and feels like straw raffia.

Scalloped Shell of straw-effect textured cloth. Veil.

Berry Pillbox of stiffly shaped veiling dotted with white "berries." Face veil.

Airy Whimsey of stiffened veil shaped like a tiny pillbox. Fancy stickpin, rayon velvet band.

Row (1) Profile deep crown Cloche; Cloche with crown full of blossoms; Envelope Pillbox; Textured straw-look Beret; High crown with deepened brim; (2) Shirred double fabric brim; Picture with cut out crown; Pleated organza Pillbox; Fabric Pillbox; (3) Scalloped Shell of straw-effect textured cloth; Pillbox of stiffened dotted netting; Pillbox shaped of stiffened netting. 1962 Sears, Roebuck and Co. catalog for Spring and Summer.

Row (1) Nylon tulle hood; Velvet crown with veiling; Nylon leaf Clip; Feather Clip; (2) Wisp of veiling; Velvet lattice ring with veiling; Headbands; Petal Half-hat; Demi-cap with dotted veil; (3) Veil with double flowers; Braid Pillbox with veil; Clip with dotted veil and bows; Bow Clip with veil. 1962 Sears, Roebuck and Co. catalog for Spring and Summer.

Hoods .. $1.99 each any 2 for $3.77

Flowering Nylon Tulle . . strewn with tiny buds. Keeps hair in place come sudden breezes.

High Crown of rayon velvet topping a puffy cage of veiling . . fits over any hairdo. Rayon velvet bow ties.

Charming Little Clips .. only $1.59 each

Wisp o' Spring . . bower of nylon leaves shaped on wire. All light and loveliness, it rests softly on your head. Made in Japan.

Side-dip Plumage . . feathers sweep down in a graceful curve for a lovely profile view. Little clip hat that fits all head sizes.

Angel's Cap, just a hint of hat as the occasion demands. A wisp of veiling and tiny fly-away bows.

Latticed Ring of rayon velvet under airy veiling . . the entire effect quite coquettish. Saucy top-knot bow.

Petal Half Hat, enchanting in silk organza petals with tiny simulated pearl buds. Made in Japan.

Saucy Bow Demi-Cap . . charming bit of feminine flippery, flattering to any woman. Straw-like cloth; chenille-dotted veil.

Lt. Mint Green
Beige
Lt. Pink
Lt. Blue
Yellow
Black
White

Head Bands 2 for $1.99

Plushy Rayon Velvet. Double fabric, contour-shaped to hug your head. Elastic in back for stay-in-place fit.

Veil with 2 lovely flowers.

Crisp Braid Pillbox. Veil.

Whimsey Clip with two rayon velvet bows. Chenille-dotted veil.

Little Bow Clip of crisp pleated cotton organdy. Eye-high veil.

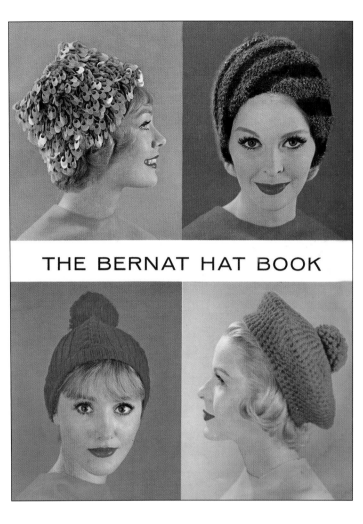

Popular and classic hat styles
to knit. 1961 Bernat Hat Book
No. 101.

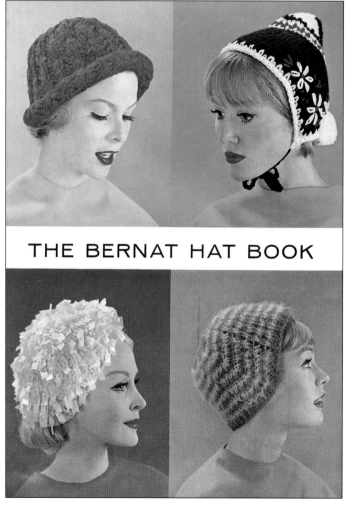

(A) Fox tail brim; (B) Mink with Rayon satin crown and cuff; (C) Plush pile Turban; (D) Cossack in faux fur; (E) Shaggy pile Turban; (F) Shaggy pile Cossack; (G) Rabbit fur Cloche; (H) Jungle spotted Turban; (J) Shaggy pile Pixie; (K) Rabbit fur hat and muff; (L) Dyed lamb Toque; (M) Pile Cloche. 1962 Sears, Roebuck and Co. catalog for Fall and Winter.

(A) Feather Toque; (B) Feather Cloche; (C) Velvet Pillbox; (D) Velvet clip with veil; (E) Felt Cloche; (F) Wispy veil with bows; (G) Satin rosette clusters; (H) Velvet button-top Pillbox; (J) Profile with pheasant feathers; (K) Feather Half-hat; (L) Mink Circlet; (M) Velvet Beret; (N) Half-hat of velvet berries. 1962 Sears, Roebuck and Co. catalog for Fall and Winter.

(A) Loopy wool Cloche; (B) Loopy knit with paillettes; (C) Wool knit Headband; (D) Looped cuff and top Cloche with paillettes; (E) Acrylic scarf Bonnet; (F) Hood with dyed lamb cuff; (G) Mohair Pixie; (H) Popcorn crochet Pillbox; (J) Cloche of sequined crocheted wool; (K) Pixie with paillettes; (L) Popcorn crochet Turban; (M) Top knot and cuff dotted with paillettes; (N) Pile Pillbox with attached scarf. 1962 Sears, Roebuck and Co. catalog for Fall and Winter.

to knit and crochet

Examples of Stocking caps, Berets, and Hoods popular at the time. 1965 Hits in Hats to Knit and Crochet.

Top Row: Hat Wigs; (1) Bulky knit Turban; (2) Acrylic Jockey Cap with attached scarf; (3) Mohair Turban; (4) Angora Turban; (5) Wool knit Jockey Cap; (6) Angora Fedora; (7) Angora Toque; (8) Angora gloves; (9) Wool knit Jester with pompon; (10) Wool mittens. 1965 Sears, Roebuck and Co. catalog for Fall and Winter.

(1) Felt Cloche; (2) Velvet ring with coque feather top-knot; (3) Velvet wide brim; (4) Velvet Toque; (5) Felt Profile; (6) Felt Casual; (7) Packable Snood; (8) Velvet Pillbox; (9) Velvet Whimsey with dotted veil; (10) Maribou feather Toque; (11) Coque feather Half-hat; (12) Feathered Pixie; (13) Metallic brocade crown Roller; (14) Chenille Roller; (15) Velvet Sailor; (16) Chenille Beret. 1965 Sears, Roebuck and Co. catalog for Fall and Winter.

(17) Wool felt Dome; (18) Oriental look Turban; (19) Packable Cloche; (20) Small brim Sailor; (21) Water repellent rain hat; (22) Felt Profile; (23) Rimmed Pillbox; (24) Velvet Jockey Cap. 1965 Sears, Roebuck and Co. catalog for Fall and Winter.

Look! Styles galore .. only $3⁹⁷

(1) Red Fox fur Hood; (2) Lamb fur Hood; (3) Rabbit fur Hood; (4)Mink tail Roller; (5) Mink Pillbox; (6) Pile Roller; (7) Rabbit fur accessories; (8) Mink tail Halo; (9) Acrylic wrap-around scarf; (10) Pile Cloche; (11) Rabbit fur Pillbox and muff. 1965 Sears, Roebuck and Co. catalog for Fall and Winter.

MOHAIR WARM UPS TO CROCHET

Left to right: Patchwork hat and scarf set;
Ripple hat and scarf set. 1967 Mohair
Warm-ups.

Popular late 1960s side brim up Fedora. 1968
Workbasket and Home Arts magazine for May.

Popular Beret and matching
sweater set. 1967 Sayelle
Yarn Book.

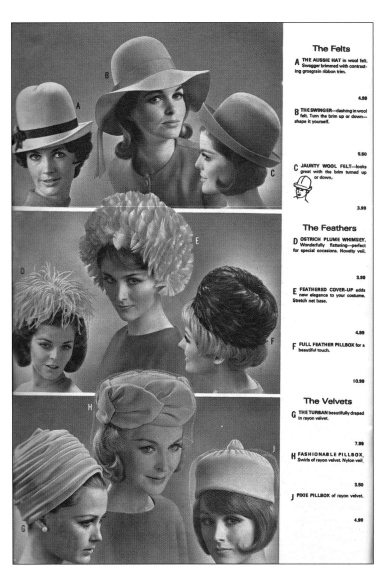

The Felts

A THE AUSSIE HAT in wool felt. Swagger brimmed with contrasting grosgrain ribbon trim.

4.99

B THE SWINGER—dashing in wool felt. Turn the brim up or down—shape it yourself.

5.50

C JAUNTY WOOL FELT—looks great with the brim turned up or down.

3.99

The Feathers

D OSTRICH PLUME WHIMSEY. Wonderfully flattering—perfect for special occasions. Novelty veil.

3.99

E FEATHERED COVER-UP adds new elegance to your costume. Stretch net base.

4.99

F FULL FEATHER PILLBOX for a beautiful touch.

10.99

The Velvets

G THE TURBAN beautifully draped in rayon velvet.

7.99

H FASHIONABLE PILLBOX. Swirls of rayon velvet. Nylon veil.

3.50

J PIXIE PILLBOX of rayon velvet.

4.99

(A) Felt Swagger; (B) Swinger with up or down brim; (C) Felt with up or down brim; (D) Ostrich plume Whimsey; (E) Feather cover-up; (F) Full feather Pillbox; (G) Velvet Turban; (H) Velvet Pillbox; (J) Velvet Pixie Pillbox. 1968 Montgomery Ward catalog for Fall and Winter.

(A) Mink Dome with tucked back; (B) Mink Pillbox; (C) Mink tail Pillbox with velvet crown; (D) Velvet ring with mink accents; (E) Mink tail Half hat; (F) Mink Dome; (G) Lamb Hood; (H) Lamb Toque. 1968 Montgomery Ward catalog for Fall and Winter.

Mink... the ultimate in luxury

A THE CROWNING TOUCH OF FASHION—sumptuous male mink skins deftly contoured in a luxurious dome shaped hat; tucked back.

54.50

B A DISTINCTIVE YOUNG DESIGN—the elegant dome pillbox exquisitely shaped of a full skin mink. Ship. wt. 1 lb.

42.50

C DAINTILY SCALED pert mink tail pillbox on rayon velvet crown fits to 23 in.

9.99

D RAYON VELVET RING with mink accents, rayon satin bow in back.

3.99

E THE MINI MINK—a half hat of mink tails with rayon satin back bow.

4.99

F GLAMOROUS DOME HAT of subtly shaded mink sides.

22.50

Look...it's lamb!

G TUSCAN LAMB HOOD—warm, weatherproof luxury. 3 tier hood; fits to 23½. Fur origin Italy.

12.99

H FASHIONABLY WINTRY—high lamb toque with an acrylic pile telescope crown.

5.99

The Great Fakeries

Fabulous pretenders play the fashion game

J JOCKY CAP

K VERSATILE 4-WAY HAT—tiered, acrylic pile crown with acrylic jersey scarf.

L THE SNUGGLER—a fur-like hood of shaggy acrylic/modacrylic pile. Pom-pom ties.

M 2-WAY HAT—close back zipper, it's a toque; open zipper, it's a hood.

N THE COSSACK TOQUE—high and handsome in a fur-like acrylic/modacrylic pile.

P FOUL WEATHER FRIEND—a cuffed hood of sheared fur-like acrylic/modacrylic.

R WARM AND DASHING—a hood of acrylic/modacrylic subtly shaded to look like fur.

T FLUFFY TURBAN

U CUDDLE CAP

(J) Acrylic Jockey cap; (K) Pile 4-way with scarf; (L) Fur-like hood; (M) Toque with back zipper to open and make it a hood; (N) Pile Cossack Toque; (P) Cuffed hood; (R) Hood of modacrylic subtly shaded to look like fur; (T) Fluffy acrylic pile Turban, (U) Fur-like cuddle cap. 1968 Montgomery Ward catalog for Fall and Winter.

(A) Celanese long fall wig; (B) Full wig; (C) Cluster of curls wig; (D) Bouffant pouf cap of curls wiglet; (E) Cascade of curls wiglet; (F) Curly stretch wig; (G) Mini fall. 1968 Montgomery Ward catalog for Fall and Winter.

A wardrobe of hairdos...

Intriguing and versatile—they swing like hair, feel like hair but behave like magic.

A-G Celanese acetate creates these quick change hairdos— soft color-fast curls with a life-like sheen that you can hand wash and reset at home. All falls attach with combs, fit all head sizes. Try several, you'll love the mini price.

(A) CLASSIC LONG FALL, a fabulous swing, abt. 20 in. 12.99

(B) LUXURIOUS FULL WIG for a marvelous quick change hairdo. It comfortably fits head sizes to 23½ in. 18.99

(C) CLUSTER OF CURLS, a specially sophisticated piece. 16.99

(D) A BOUFFANT POUF cap with the prettiest curls. 7.49

(E) A CASCADE OF CURLS, gloriously romantic. Abt. 8". 6.99

(F) CURLY STRETCH WIG—the season's newest look mounted on a soft, comfortable stretch cap. 22.50

(G) MINI FALL, fashion's new shorter look. Abt. 5". 9.99

HAT shown on fig. E. Feathered bow of rayon velvet. 3.00

Beret examples to knit and crochet. 1968 Stoles - Hats - Scarfs to knit or crochet.

The PILLBOX

Soft, rayon plush (cotton-backed) in a wild print .. looks like expensive leopard fur.

$5.97

Plush leopard print Pillbox. 1968 Sears, Roebuck and Co. catalog for Fall and Winter.

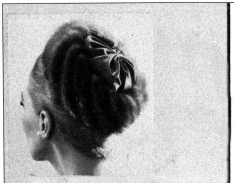

The FUR PILLBOX

5 A circle of natural mink tails .. topped with rayon satin.

$7.00

Mink tail Pillbox. 1968 Sears, Roebuck and Co. catalog for Fall and Winter.

SNAP-BRIM HAT

Wool felt.

$6.90

Snap brim felt. 1968 Sears, Roebuck and Co. catalog for Fall and Winter.

Mink Toque. 1968 Sears, Roebuck and Co. catalog for Fall and Winter.

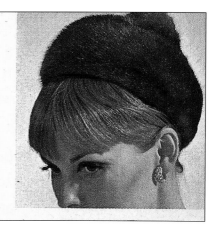

NATURAL MINK TOQUE

Prime, plump full pelt .. truly luxurious.

$39.90

Cable stitch knit Helmet. 1968 Sears, Roebuck and Co. catalog for Fall and Winter.

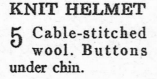

KNIT HELMET

5 Cable-stitched wool. Buttons under chin.

$3.97

Linen-look sectional Beret. 1969 Sears, Roebuck and Co. catalog for Spring and Summer.

The BERET

Sewn sections .. fabric of flax, rayon and cotton looks like linen. Lined.

$5.50

Linen-look snap brim. 1969 Sears, Roebuck and Co. catalog for Spring and Summer.

STITCHED-BRIM HAT

Flax, rayon and cotton fabric looks like linen. Brim turns up or down. Button-and-loop trim.

$5.97

Our fake furs are real fashion

A WIDE BRIMMED CLOCHE goes to your head in a very flattering way. Mink-look acrylic-modacrylic pile.

11.00

B BAG shoulders the load in "rich girl" style. Of acrylic-modacrylic pile in colors to match the mink-look hats shown this page. Rayon lined. Size: abt. 12x10½".

7.00

C SMALL BRIMMED CLOCHE adds a smart finishing touch to cold weather outfits. Mink-look acrylic-modacrylic pile.

8.00

D HIGH CROWNED TOQUE comes out on top in this season's fashion game. Choose mink-look or raccoon-look pile of acrylic-modacrylic.

5.00

E JOCKEY CAP hits a jaunty high note with its perky pompon styling. Ear-warming stretch cuff and visor are acrylic knit. Available in raccoon-look or mink-look pile of acrylic-modacrylic.

5.00

F "COSSACK" TOQUE heads into the coldest day in high style. Lamb-look pile of acrylic-modacrylic.

6.00

G SINGLE TIERED TOQUE heads off winter chills. Sleek seal-look acrylic pile.

6.50

Hand-crocheted styles look so smart

H CAP has the boldly knit look that's tops this season. Deep cuff for ear-covering warmth. Hand-crocheted of soft acrylic. Hand wash, cold. Fits to 23 inches.

L 5 A 6765 . . . . 6.00

LOW PRICE FOR AN ACRYLIC TURBAN $3

J TURBAN is styled with a flattering criss-cross front. It stretches to cover hair and ears. Hand crocheted acrylic. Hand wash, cold. Fits to 23". Made in Japan.

L 5 A 6703—State color number . . . 3.00

(A) Fake fur wide brim Cloche; (B) Shoulder bag; (C) Small brim Cloche; (D) High crowned Toque; (E) Jockey cap; (F) Cossack Toque; (G) Single tiered Toque; (H) Bold knit Cap with deep cuff; (J) Stretch crochet Turban. 1974 Montgomery Ward catalog for Fall and Winter.

(A) Rabbit fur Toque; (B) Lamb Cloche; (C) Lamb Hood; (D) Round crown visor Cap; (E) Furry Tote; (F) Modacrylic ponytail braid wiglet; (G) Cluster curl wiglet; (H) Flexible curly wiglet; (J) Curl cluster wiglet. 1974 Montgomery Ward catalog for Fall and Winter.

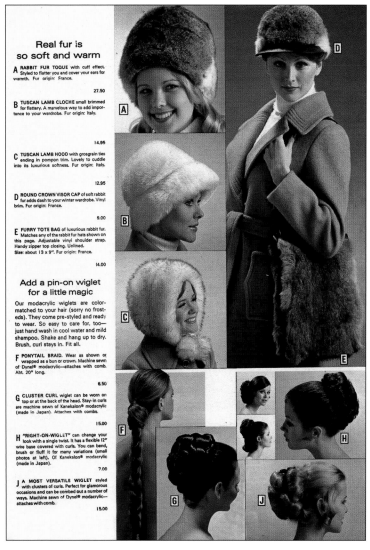

Real fur is so soft and warm

A RABBIT FUR TOQUE with cuff effect. Styled to flatter you and cover your ears for warmth. Fur origin: France.

27.50

B TUSCAN LAMB CLOCHE small brimmed for flattery. A marvelous way to add importance to your wardrobe. Fur origin: Italy.

14.95

C TUSCAN LAMB HOOD with grosgrain ties ending in pompon trim. Lovely to cuddle into its luxurious softness. Fur origin: Italy.

12.95

D ROUND CROWN VISOR CAP of soft rabbit fur adds dash to your winter wardrobe. Vinyl brim. Fur origin: France.

9.00

E FURRY TOTE BAG of luxurious rabbit fur. Matches any of the rabbit fur hats shown on this page. Adjustable vinyl shoulder strap. Handy zipper top closing. Unlined. Size: about 13 x 9". Fur origin: France.

14.00

Add a pin-on wiglet for a little magic

Our modacrylic wiglets are color-matched to your hair (sorry no frost-eds). They come pre-styled and ready to wear. So easy to care for, too— just hand wash in cool water and mild shampoo. Shake and hang up to dry. Brush, curl stays in. Fit all.

F PONYTAIL BRAID. Wear as shown or wrapped as a bun or crown. Machine sewn of Dynel® modacrylic—attaches with comb. Abt. 20" long.

6.50

G CLUSTER CURL wiglet can be worn on top or at the back of the head. Stay-in curls are machine sewn of Kanekalon® modacrylic (made in Japan). Attaches with comb.

15.00

H "RIGHT-ON-WIGLET" can change your look with a single twist. It has a flexible 12" wire base covered with curls. You can bend, brush or fluff it for many variations (small photos at left). Of Kanekalon® modacrylic (made in Japan).

7.00

J A MOST VERSATILE WIGLET styled with clusters of curls. Perfect for glamorous occasions and can be combed out a number of ways. Machine sewn of Dynel® modacrylic—attaches with comb.

15.00

BIBLIOGRAPHY

Advance Pattern Company #4655, 1947.
Aldens Catalog, Spring & Summer 1952.
Bernat Handicrafter #101 *Hat Book*, 1961.
Chicago Mail Order Catalog, 1927.
Chicago Mail Order Catalog, 1931.
Chicago Mail Order Catalog, 1933.
Chicago Mail Order Catalog, 1935.
Chicago Mail Order Catalog, 1939.
Dawn Sayelle. "Knitted and Crocheted Fashions #188."
   American Thread, c. 1967.
Fine Millinery Catalog, Spring and Summer 1904.
Hand Crochet Fashions by Dritz, 1953.
Hits in Hats to Knit and Crochet, Vol. 92, 1965.
Home Needlework Magazine, June 1915.
Ideas for Gifts, Clark's J & P Coats Book #255, 1949.
Metropolitan by F. Butterick & Co., December 1872.
Modern Priscilla Magazine, January 1909.
Modern Priscilla Magazine, April 1909.
Modern Priscilla Magazine, November 1909.
Modern Priscilla Magazine, January 1910.
Modern Priscilla Magazine, March 1910.
Modern Priscilla Magazine, April 1910.
Modern Priscilla Magazine, May 1910.
Modern Priscilla Magazine, August 1910.
Modern Priscilla Magazine, September 1910.
Modern Priscilla Magazine, October 1910.
Modern Priscilla Magazine, February 1916.
Modern Priscilla Magazine, July 1916.
Modern Priscilla Magazine, October 1916.
Modernes Journal fur Deutsche Frauen, c. 1900.
Montgomery Ward Catalog, 1916.
Montgomery Ward Catalog, Spring & Summer 1923.
Montgomery Ward Catalog, 1925.
Montgomery Ward #4 Sale Catalog, 1927.
Montgomery Ward August 31 Sale Catalog, 1928.
Montgomery Ward Sale Catalog, 1929.
Montgomery Ward Book 3 Sale Catalog, 1928.
Montgomery Ward Sale Catalog, 1929.
Montgomery Ward Book 1 Sale Catalog, 1929.
Montgomery Ward Catalog, 1929.
Montgomery Ward #1 Sale Catalog, 1930.
Montgomery Ward 2-28 Sale Catalog, 1930.
Montgomery Ward Book 6 Sale Catalog, 1930.

Montgomery Ward Unload Sale Catalog, 1930.
Montgomery Ward Sale Catalog. c. early 1930s.
Montgomery Ward Book 3 Sale Catalog, 1931.
Montgomery Ward Book 2A Sale Catalog, 1932.
Montgomery Ward Catalog, 1934.
Montgomery Ward February Sale Catalog, 1934.
Montgomery Ward April 30 Sale Catalog, 1934.
Montgomery Ward Spring & Summer Sale Catalog, 1934.
Montgomery Ward June 15 Sale Catalog, 1934.
Montgomery Ward August 31 Sale Catalog, 1934.
Montgomery Ward July Sale Catalog, 1935.
Montgomery Ward Catalog, Spring & Summer 1938.
Montgomery Ward Catalog, Fall & Winter 1939-40.
Montgomery Ward Catalog, Fall & Winter 1941-42.
Montgomery Ward Catalog, Spring & Summer 1945.
Montgomery Ward Catalog, Fall & Winter 1947-48.
Montgomery Ward Catalog, Fall & Winter 1949-50.
Montgomery Ward Catalog, Fall & Winter 1951-52.
Montgomery Ward Catalog, Spring & Summer 1953.
Montgomery Ward Catalog, Fall & Winter 1955-56.
Montgomery Ward Catalog, Fall & Winter 1958-59.
Montgomery Ward Catalog, 1968.
Montgomery Ward Catalog, Fall & Winter 1974.
National Bellas Hess Catalog, 1930.
National Bellas Hess Catalog, 1931.
National Cloak & Suit Company Catalog, 1913.
National Cloak & Suit Company Catalog, Spring & Summer 1927.
Needlework, The Magazine of Home Arts, September 1931.
Needlework, The Magazine of Home Arts, November 1934.
Peoples Popular Magazine, 1927.
Pictoral Review Magazine, 1907.
Pictoral Fashion Book, Summer 1938.
Sears, Roebuck and Co. Consumers Guide, Fall 1900. Northfield,
   IL: DBI Books, 1970.
Sears, Roebuck and Co. Consumers Guide, Spring 1902. New
   York: Crown Publishers, 1969.
Sears, Roebuck and Co. Catalog, 1916-17.
Sears, Roebuck and Co. Catalog, Spring & Summer 1921.
Sears, Roebuck and Co. Catalog, Fall & Winter 1928-29.
Sears, Roebuck and Co. Catalog, 1934.
Sears, Roebuck and Co. Fall Money Saver Sale Catalog, 1936.
Sears, Roebuck and Co. Catalog, Spring & Summer 1939.
Sears, Roebuck and Co. Catalog, Spring & Summer 1940.

Sears, Roebuck and Co. Catalog, Fall & Winter 1944-45.
Sears, Roebuck and Co. Catalog, Fall & Winter 1948.
Sears, Roebuck and Co. Catalog, Spring & Summer 1949.
Sears, Roebuck and Co. Catalog, Fall & Winter 1956.
Sears, Roebuck and Co. Catalog, Spring & Summer 1956.
Sears, Roebuck and Co. Catalog, Spring & Summer 1962.
Sears, Roebuck and Co. Catalog, Fall & Winter 1962.
Sears, Roebuck and Co. Catalog, Fall & Winter 1965.
Sears, Roebuck and Co. Catalog, Fall & Winter 1968.
Sears, Roebuck and Co. Catalog, Spring & Summer 1969.

Stoles - Hats - Scarfs to Knit or Crochet, Vol 14 . 1968.
The Delinator, E. B. Butterick & Co., 1896.
The Ladies World, August 1905.
W. & H. Walker Catalog, Fall & Winter 1913-14.
Wacs and Waves Cut Out Dolls. Racine, WI: Whitman Publishing, 1943.
Wichita Beacon Newspaper, July 3, 1927.
Woman's Home Companion, November 1904.
The Workbasket and Home Arts Magazine #8, Vol 33, May 1968.

INDEX OF HAT STYLES